Hoxton Street Monster Supplies

ESTᴰ 1818

~ *Purveyor of Quality Goods for Monsters of Every Kind* ~

DEAD GOOD

MANY OF OUR CUSTOMERS
HAVE BEEN COMING TO US FOR CENTURIES

SOME FOR CONSIDERABLY LONGER

www.monstersupplies.org

For Igor

—

*A Disgustingly
Discerning
Founder
and
Monster Assistant
Extraordinaire*

THE
MONSTER'S COOKBOOK

EVERYDAY RECIPES FOR
THE LIVING, DEAD, AND UNDEAD

MITCHELL
BEAZLEY

— Revised edition featuring recipes suitable for humans —

CONTENTS

INTRODUCTION

Three thousand years ago, a dinner invitation from a Troll or a Cyclops would have been unheard of. Monster communities were physically spread out and many lived a hand-to-mouth existence, hunting animals on the plains, and occasionally venturing into settlements to prey on humans. The only nod toward culinary expertise was the fire pit—essentially a means of warmth but also used to cook tougher cuts of meat.

Luckily, times have changed—transportation links, monster markets, refrigeration (for maintaining the optimum level of decay), and a bounty of health and cookery literature have resulted in monsters elevating food from its lowly status of survival fodder to something that is eagerly anticipated and enjoyed. Menus are now planned in advance, ingredients are carefully chosen, and friends and family gather together to enjoy meals socially.

PROVENANCE

Monsters have become savvier with regard to where ingredients are sourced and produced. A surge in the popularity of organic human dismemberers, free-range farms, and ethically sourced body parts led to the closure of many factory farms in the last century, with suppliers forced to disclose the provenance of every last toenail and brain. There has also been a rise in the number of homotarians—Swamp Creatures and more enlightened Vampires, in particular, are choosing to embrace a human-meat-free lifestyle and form bonds of friendship with humans rather than serving them up for dinner.

ALLERGIES AND DIETARY REQUIREMENTS

As well as ensuring the quality of ingredients, many home cooks also have to contend with the increase in allergies and food intolerances, particularly among monster offspring. It is believed this is largely due to a generation of fast-food humans entering the food chain (specimens with fat-clogged arteries are now strictly prohibited for monster consumption and can only be sold as minions).

In the meantime, allergy sufferers need to steer clear of certain ingredients that could cause a reaction. Common conditions include: hair fever, pus intolerance, human-dander allergy, blood boils, and eyeball dermatitis. It is advised to always check the labels of prepackaged body parts; if in doubt, buy a whole carcass from a reputable retailer and ask your local dismemberer to break it down for you.

USING THE BOOK

As more monsters indulge their passion for cuisine, they are increasingly looking for recipe ideas for home cooking and entertaining. This collection of sweet and savory dishes has taken traditional community favorites and updated them for the modern gourmand. With ingredients such as winter-flu pus, organic swamp water, Neanderthal guts, and fairy brains now very difficult—or impossible—to source, centuries-old family favorites have dropped off the dinner menu. This revised edition of the cookbook is also suitable for humans looking to expand on their recipe repertoire.

The modern monster has a poor work–life balance: Zombies take twice as long to perform any task; Vampires work long night shifts; Swamp Creatures have very long commutes; and Giant Apes are dealing with deforestation. Everyone is looking for quick-fix snacks with accessible ingredients and, whether you're gut intolerant, human-friendly, or follow a gluten-free or bone-restricted diet, you'll find plenty of inspiration in this book.

From party classics such as Strawberry Shortdeads (see page 52) to lunchtime liveners like Classic Orphan Marmalade (see page 97), you'll soon be wooing Werewolves, tempting Trolls, delighting Dragons, and introducing Vampires to a whole host of bloodless midnight snacks.

ABOUT THE SHOP

If you happen to be strolling around the streets of East London, you might chance upon this splendidly appointed yet delightfully unassuming shopfront. Monsters have been crossing the threshold of Hoxton Street Monster Supplies since the shop opened back in 1818, with the local human population largely oblivious to the nocturnal comings and goings of the capital's Vampires, Zombies, Dragons, Sasquatches, and Trolls.

Behind the traditional façade lies a wealth of everyday items for the living, dead, and undead. As the only purveyor of monster supplies in London (and possibly in the world), we're proud of our long history of helping the monster community thrive in the heart of the city. From sweet treats like Cubed Earwax, to gifts like Bah! Humbugs and Banshee Balls, this one-stop monster supply shop caters to every taste, whim, and fancy.

One of our primary aims is to help our clientele navigate through the increasingly tricky terrain of the modern world, and to ensure that their traditional way of life isn't threatened and their culture is respected and protected. Our range of carefully crafted products, including Tinned Fear and Salt Made From Tears, enables customers to continue scaring, hunting, shape shifting, transmogrifying, and reanimating with impunity.

THE HISTORY OF THE SHOP

Though the history of our shop is distinctly murky, we are fairly confident that Hoxton Street Monster Supplies was founded by Igor, the celebrated personal assistant to both Victor Frankenstein and Count Dracula. He subsequently worked closely with several other notable monsters, but after a tragic incident with a vat of snot found himself out of work. He fled Transylvania, and arrived in London in 1817.

His previous career meant Igor was a fount of knowledge when it came to remedies, personal grooming, and fine consumables. He soon became a major player on the London monster social scene, with monsters traveling far and wide to ask him to procure hard-to-find remedies and groceries. Igor spotted a gap in the market and opened the shop on Hoxton Street. It quickly became a convening point for London's monster community—providing much-needed social contact, insider information on good scaring locations, and, naturally, the finest range of gourmet monster groceries in the capital.

Fast-forward to 2010 when we completely overhauled and modernized the interior. Hundreds of years of cobwebs were cleared, electricity was installed, and we even set up a website. Perhaps most controversially, the shop became fully visible and accessible to human customers.

Naturally, many of the older generation of monster clientele were alarmed by these sudden and dramatic changes. But they quickly appreciated not having to wear reading glasses when browsing the shelves, and being able to shop online during inclement weather.

THE CURSE OF CREATIVITY

Due to a rather inconvenient curse, all our profits go to the Ministry of Stories, a creative writing and mentoring charity for young humans. We are doing everything in our power to rectify this intolerable situation.

Golden Rules for Entertaining

Whether it's a family gathering or a dinner party for friends, the diverse dietary, social, and cultural requirements of different members of the community mean that careful planning must take place before any event. From sending out invitations (large print for Cyclopses; simplified text for Zombies; voicemail for illiterate Giant Apes and Swamp Creatures), to choosing the menu and entertainment, social gatherings can be a balancing act of epic proportions. So, while it is perfectly possible to host a party with an eclectic guest list, it is advisable to follow a few simple guidelines for a successful celebration.

☞ If Vampires are on the guest list, be sure to start proceedings after dark and keep garlic *firmly off* the ingredients list—if possible, out of the house completely. You might also want to advise any human guests to wear a scarf or turtleneck sweater: Vampires can be very restrained in social situations but you don't want to risk temptation after a couple of aperitifs.

☞ If your party falls during a full moon, adjust the catering accordingly: Werewolves have *particularly voracious* appetites at this time and can devour twice the regular portion size of each course.

☞ Zombies take things *very slowly* so allow extra time for dinner and niceties. It is also advised to plan a simple menu around these guests—they're not the sharpest tools in the box and anything too complicated could quickly use up the few remaining brain cells they possess.

☞ *Under no circumstances* should you seat a Cyclops next to a Giant Spider. Despite their size, Cyclopses tend to be sensitive about their solitary eye and they might construe the seating plan as an underhand insult.

☞ If you have small humans, think carefully before inviting Under-the-Bed or In-the-Cupboard Monsters to your soirée. Although they rarely mix work with pleasure, they can *sometimes* mistake the suggestion of after-dinner party games as an open invitation to scare children witless in the name of light entertainment.

☞ Keep Swamp Creatures off the guest list if you've recently had new carpets fitted. Some hosts offer slime-proof onesies on arrival but there will inevitably be a certain amount of *leakage* during the course of the evening.

☞ Dragons and Yetis should be seated at *opposite ends* of the table for obvious reasons of temperature control—a hot Yeti does not make for a convivial dinner guest. If they do get a little flushed, open the freezer door and perch them in front of it for half an hour.

☞ Zombies are *very self-conscious* about shedding errant limbs and will often turn down dinner invitations for fear of dropping a finger into a fondue or losing a leg during a game of Twister. You can pre-empt this by supplying a large box or re-useable shopping bag, in which they can deposit loose limbs and collect them when they leave.

Hoxton Street Monster Supplies

ESTᴰ 1818

~ Purveyor of Quality Goods for Monsters of Every Kind ~

SWEETS
&
PASTILLES

INCLUDING

CRUNCHING BONE TOFFEE

& FAIRY BRAIN FUDGE

CRUNCHING BONE TOFFEE

In days gone by, Bone Toffee was a particular favorite of Werewolves and Giants, as the mouth-watering combination of lightly crushed human bones and sweet toffee was a rare treat. If you're a stickler for the classics and can source human bones, you can ask your local human dismemberer to crunch them for you. If not, we're confident you'll find our 21st-century version of the recipe most agreeable.

Sufficient.—for 6 oz of toffee

about 2 oz milk chocolate,
    broken into pieces
2 oz firm toffees
¼ cup milk
1 tablespoon vegetable oil
½ cup popcorn kernels

Method.—Melt the chocolate in a small heatproof bowl set over a small saucepan of gently simmering water.

Meanwhile, unwrap the toffees and put them in a polythene bag. Place on a cutting board and tap firmly with a rolling pin until the toffees have broken into small pieces. Tip the pieces into a small saucepan and add the milk. Cook on the lowest possible heat until the toffee has melted (this will take several minutes, depending on the firmness of the toffee). Remove from the heat.

Put the oil in a large saucepan with a tight-fitting lid and heat for 1 minute. Add the popcorn kernels and cover with the lid. Cook until the popping sound stops, then tip the popcorn out onto a large baking pan or roasting pan and let cool for 5 minutes.

Using a teaspoon, drizzle lines of the toffee sauce over the popcorn until lightly coated. Drizzle with lines of the melted chocolate in the same way.

CRUNCHING BONE TOFFEE

Try if you can to source your humans from around gyms and exercise clubs.
Their strong, healthy bones provide a pleasant crunch.

BLOODSUCKER PASTILLES

The freshest human blood was traditionally used to achieve the soft, gooey consistency of these pastilles. They were commonly prepared for baby monsters during weaning, as they could use their gums to chew and gain an early bloodlust. This updated version is no less delicious—serve them as a sweet snack to elderly family members who no longer have the luxury of a full set of fangs.

Sufficient.—for about 25 pastilles

1 tablespoon vegetable oil or sunflower oil,
    plus extra for oiling
¾ lb strawberries, hulled
¾-inch thick slice of lemon, rind and any
    seeds removed
2 cups jam sugar
2 tablespoons superfine sugar

Method.—Line a 6-inch square dish with parchment paper and grease with the oil. Blitz the strawberries and lemon slice in a food processor or blender, then press the mixture through a fine sieve into a stainless steel pan.

Add the jam sugar and mix well, then place over medium heat and bring to a boil. When the mixture is bubbling vigorously, cook for 35 minutes, stirring occasionally, until thick and a little darker in color. Pour carefully into the prepared dish and let cool for about 1 hour.

Lift out of the dish and peel off the paper, then cut the mixture into about 25 pastilles using a lightly oiled mini metal cookie cutter. Alternatively, lightly oil a large, sharp knife and cut into small squares. Spread the superfine sugar on a plate, then roll each pastille in the sugar until coated, brushing away any excess.

AFTER-GORGING BREATH MINTS

These mints will help solve the age-old conundrum of rancid breath following a brain banquet, so keep a few handy at dinner parties and on first dates. Nothing quite dampens the ardor of a Zombie suitor like human-organ halitosis: a quick suck on a breath mint will greatly improve your chances of some undead corporeal carousing.

Sufficient.—for about 100 mints

1½ cups sifted confectioners' sugar,
    plus extra for dusting
2 tablespoons butter, melted
1 to 2 teaspoons peppermint extract
1 to 2 teaspoons milk
few drops of green or blue food
    coloring (optional)

Method.—Place the confectioners' sugar, butter, and peppermint extract in a large bowl and mix to combine to a stiff but not sticky mixture, adding a splash of milk, if necessary. Add more peppermint to taste, if needed.

Tip the peppermint mixture onto a surface dusted with confectioners' sugar and add the food coloring, if using. Knead for 1 minute until smooth.

Divide the mixture into 4 pieces, then roll each into a long, thin sausage. Cut into ½-inch pieces and shape into large-blueberry-sized balls (or make them as small or as big as you like).

Roll the balls in extra sifted confectioners' sugar, then leave, uncovered, until firm. Store in an airtight can or jar for up to 1 week.

FAIRY BRAIN FUDGE

Fairy brains used to be notoriously difficult to harvest, which made them expensive. In days gone by, connoisseurs would cut costs by hanging around outside human houses at night-time, waiting for the fairies to come out after collecting unwanted teeth. The delicate consistency of the tiny brains transformed the simple fudge recipe into a luxurious treat. Nowadays, most tribes share the human sweet tooth and sugar is preferred, so this recipe has replaced the original.

Sufficient.—for 36 pieces of fudge

1 stick butter, plus extra
  for greasing
1 cup evaporated milk
2¼ cups superfine sugar
3 tablespoons water

2 teaspoons vanilla extract
3 oz semisweet chocolate,
  chopped
8 oreo cookies or bourbon
  biscuits, chopped

Method.—Put the butter, evaporated milk, sugar, measured water, and vanilla extract in a heavy saucepan and heat gently, stirring, until the sugar has dissolved. Bring to a boil and then let the mixture boil for 10 minutes, stirring constantly. Test to see if it is ready by carefully dropping ½ teaspoon of the mixture into some cold water—it should form a soft ball.

Pour half the fudge mixture quickly into a heatproof pitcher. Add the chocolate to the remaining fudge mixture in the pan and stir to melt.

Pour half the chocolate fudge into a greased 8½ x 4½ inch loaf pan, then carefully scatter with half the cookies. Pour the vanilla fudge on top and scatter with the remainder of the cookies. Finish with a final layer of chocolate fudge. Let cool, then cover with plastic wrap and chill overnight.

Invert the fudge onto a board and cut into 36 pieces.

FAIRY BRAIN FUDGE

If using real fairies, be sure to pick out any teeth that they have collected—keep them aside, and sprinkle on a bowl of mucus porridge for added crunch.

TURKISH DESPAIR

This store cupboard staple will swiftly reverse the agonizing side effects of a bout of optimism or goodwill. Prepare a few batches at once and keep them wrapped in parchment (human-skin parchment was traditionally used) in a cool, dry place. Optimism can be highly contagious—particularly among the elderly and infirm—so it's best to nip it in the bud as soon as you notice any feelings of euphoria.

Sufficient.—for about 30 to 40 pieces of despair

1 tablespoon vegetable oil or sunflower
    oil, plus extra for oiling
¾ lb strawberries, hulled
¾-inch thick slice of lemon, rind and
    any seeds removed

2 cups jam sugar
2 tablespoons rosewater
⅓ cup superfine sugar or confectioners'
    sugar (or a mixture of the two),
    for dusting

Method.—Line a 6-inch square dish with parchment paper and grease with the oil. Blitz the strawberries and lemon slice in a food processor or blender, then press the mixture through a fine sieve into a stainless steel pan.

Add the jam sugar and 1 tablespoon of the rosewater and mix well. Place over medium heat and bring to a boil. When the mixture is bubbling vigorously, cook for 35 minutes, stirring occasionally, until thick and a little darker in color. Add the remaining rosewater and cook for a further 2 minutes. Pour carefully into the prepared dish and let cool for about 1 hour.

Lift out of the dish and peel off the paper, then cut into ¾-inch squares (or any size you like) using a lightly oiled large, sharp knife. Dust the top of the squares with the superfine or confectioners' sugar.

MIDNIGHT DROPS

Humans and monsters alike thrive during a full moon, but Vampires and Werewolves rely more heavily on its restorative powers. A couple of Midnight Drops after dinner will ensure you harness every last ounce of lunar energy. Werewolves can double the dose for seamless shape shifting but humans should ingest with care, as overindulgence can result in fatal flatulence.

Sufficient.—for 24 drops

1 cup heavy cream
13 oz semisweet chocolate, broken
   into pieces

3 to 4 tablespoons brandy or rum
   (optional)
2 tablespoons cocoa powder, sifted
crystallized violets, to decorate

Method.—Pour the cream into a small saucepan and bring to a boil. Remove from the heat and stir in 7 ounces of the chocolate. Let stand until melted, then stir in the brandy or rum, if using, and mix until smooth. Chill for 4 hours until the truffle mixture is firm.

Line a cookie sheet with nonstick parchment paper and dust with the cocoa powder. Scoop a little truffle mixture into a teaspoon, then transfer it to a second spoon and back to the first again, making a well rounded egg shape (or use a melon baller). Slide the drop onto the cocoa-dusted paper. Repeat until all the mixture is used up. Chill again for 2 hours, or overnight if possible, until firm.

Melt the remaining chocolate in a heatproof bowl set over a saucepan of gently simmering water. Stir well, then, holding 1 Midnight Drop at a time on a fork over a bowl, spoon melted chocolate over the top to coat it. Place the drops on a piece of nonstick parchment paper on a cookie sheet. Swirl a little chocolate over the top of each with a spoon and decorate with a crystallized violet.

Chill for at least 1 hour, then pack into paper petit-four cups and arrange in a gift box.

DRAGON FUEL

If you're acquainted with a Dragon that's not firing on all cylinders, drop by with a gift of these chili-laced fuel drops to help speed up recovery and restore them to full flame power. They're more effective than a posset or potion but take heed—they are highly potent—too many in one sitting and your flame-throwing friend is liable to set every lair in the locality ablaze.

Sufficient.—for 25 pieces of fuel

¾ cup heavy cream
2 tablespoons butter
5 oz semisweet chocolate, chopped
pinch of chili powder, plus extra
    to serve (optional)
¾ cup cocoa powder

Method.—Put the cream and butter in a small saucepan and heat until the butter melts and the mixture is simmering. Place the chocolate in a heatproof bowl and pour over the hot cream. Add the chili powder and stir together until the chocolate melts. Chill for at least 4 hours until firm.

Using a melon baller or lightly oiled hands, shape the chocolate mixture into 25 small walnut-sized balls. Spread the cocoa powder on a plate, then roll each chocolate ball in the cocoa until well coated.

Transfer to individual paper candy cups or arrange on a plate and serve, dusted with a little extra chili powder, if liked.

DRAGON FUEL

CAUTION

*Consumption by non-Dragons may result in a long, painful, and fiery death—
or mild indigestion, depending on your species.*

Diet & Lifestyle

Food provenance has become increasingly important to discerning *bon viveurs*. Mealtimes are no longer simply an opportunity to refuel—raw ingredients are carefully sourced and put together, as flesh-eating communities enjoy more social dining, and are acknowledging the link between healthy eating and longevity. The rise in allergies has also prompted an interest in specialist diets—juice and organic bone bars have been springing up all over the place and you can't move in monster markets for the range of low-carb and gluten-free ready meals.

FREE-RANGE AND GM FREE

These days it is possible for flesh-eaters to entirely avoid GM and factory-farmed humans. Home cooks can buy directly from organic shops and human farmers' markets, where cuts are ethically sourced. Some individuals still prefer to hunt their own humans but obviously there's no guarantee that they've been following an organic diet—there is a high risk of fast-food contamination.

GLUTEN FREE

If you suffer from gluten intolerance it is best to avoid nationalities that have bread or pasta as staple foods. Gluten-free humans come at a premium so always check the provenance carefully. Any pasty-looking specimens carrying extra weight should arouse your suspicions, as should those with jam around the mouth or on the fingers—a sure sign that bread was consumed shortly before death.

RAW FOOD

Swamp Creatures and Zombies are the original raw foodists but other members of the community have jumped on the bandwagon in the name of health and well being. Purists won't let any part of their human store cupboard go near the fire pit—the idea being that the nutritional value remains intact if the food is eaten raw. Classic recipes include human tartare with a raw dragon egg, and bile juice topped with ground bonemeal.

LOW CARB

If you or your guests are following a low-carb diet, you should avoid serving the fattier human cuts and instead stick to organs and variety meats. The largely sedentary life of Giants and Mummies has led to many being advised by their physicians to cut down on carbs. So, if you have any Giants coming to dinner, it's best to play it safe by serving fish or vegetable dishes. If you can't resist offering a few carb-laden accompaniments, you could subtly suggest working out to a celebrity fitness DVD after dinner to help your guests shed a few calories.

THE 5:2 DIET

This latest diet craze is easy to follow so Zombies, in particular, have been keen to adopt it. Dieters basically just consume swamp water for two days a week and then eat regular meals for the other five days. There has been some controversy relating to the diet, as members of the Giant community hadn't realized it was a weight-loss diet rather than a lifestyle choice—it proved so successful that they slimmed down and can no longer shake the earth when they jump.

Hoxton Street Monster Supplies

ESTᴰ 1818

~ Purveyor of Quality Goods for Monsters of Every Kind ~

BISCUITS & COOKIES

INCLUDING

GINGERDEAD MEN

& BURSTING BOIL BISCUITS

COARSELY GROUND BONE BISCUITS

Organic bone flour was traditionally the ingredient of choice for this classic recipe, as the humans weren't fed junk food. However, when bone flour rationing came into effect, and it was almost impossible to source organic, this easy alternative using wheat flour was introduced. These make great after-school snacks for the young ones— double the quantity for Giant offspring or very hungry Ogres.

Sufficient.—for 18 to 20 biscuits

½ cup crunchy peanut butter
½ cup superfine sugar
½ stick slightly salted butter,
    softened, plus extra for greasing
1 egg, lightly beaten
1 cup all-purpose flour, sifted with
    1 teaspoon baking powder
¼ cup salted peanuts, chopped

Method.—Beat together the peanut butter, sugar, and butter in a bowl until well combined. Add the egg and flour and mix to a paste.

Roll teaspoonfuls of the mixture into 18 to 20 small walnut-sized balls, then place slightly apart on a large greased cookie sheet and flatten with a fork. Scatter the biscuits with the chopped peanuts.

Bake in a preheated oven at 350°F for 18 to 20 minutes until risen and deep golden. Transfer to a wire rack to cool.

COARSELY GROUND BONE BISCUITS

The inherent crunchiness of bones makes these unsuitable for
the brittle teeth, fangs, or tusks of older monsters.

PHLEGMY DODGERS

This recipe is a rework of a classic that featured phlegm as the star ingredient. If you want to try the original, it's worth noting that humans tend to suffer from nasty coughs and colds during the winter, so this is the optimum time to harvest good-quality phlegm. It can be stored in sterilized jars for up to three months; just stir before use, as green and yellow phlegm tends to separate.

Sufficient.—for 16 dodgers

2¼ cups all-purpose flour, plus extra
    for dusting
1¾ sticks chilled unsalted butter,
    diced, plus extra for greasing
1 cup sifted confectioners' sugar
2 egg yolks
2 teaspoons vanilla bean paste
¼ cup strawberry jam or lemon curd

Buttercream
1¼ cups sifted confectioners' sugar
¾ stick unsalted butter, softened
1 teaspoon hot water

Method.—Place the flour in a bowl or food processor. Add the butter and rub in with the fingertips or process until the mixture resembles bread crumbs. Add the sugar, egg yolks, and vanilla bean paste and mix or blend to a smooth dough. Seal in plastic wrap and chill for at least 1 hour.

Roll out the dough on a lightly floured surface. Cut out 32 disks using a 2½-inch plain cookie cutter. Place slightly apart on 2 greased cookie sheets. Cut eyes and a smiling mouth (fangs optional) into half of the cookies, using a small, sharp knife.

Bake in a preheated oven at 350°F for 15 minutes or until pale golden. Transfer to a wire rack to cool.

Make the buttercream. Beat together the confectioners' sugar, butter, and measured water until smooth and creamy. Spread the buttercream onto the plain cookies, then spread with the jam or lemon curd. Gently press the face cookies on top.

INDIGESTIVES

Yetis, Swamp Creatures, and Giants from the Northern Hemisphere used to rely on indigestibles to get them through the harsh winters. Almost impossible to digest, they would keep hungry predators full until the mountain passes cleared and the human hunting season began. However, since online grocery shopping reached the remotest locales, there was no need to force down the foul snacks and this delicious biscuit took its place in the cookie barrel.

Sufficient.—for 18 to 22 indigestives

1 stick unsalted butter, softened
1 teaspoon vanilla bean paste or extract
1 cup superfine sugar
1 large egg, lightly beaten
½ cup mixed chopped nuts
1½ cups all-purpose flour

1 teaspoon cream of tartar
½ teaspoon baking powder
2 teaspoons ground cinnamon
pinch of ground nutmeg
¼ teaspoon salt

Method.—Line 2 cookie sheets with nonstick parchment paper. Beat together the butter, vanilla, and ¾ cup of the sugar in a bowl until light and fluffy. Add the egg and beat well, then stir in the chopped nuts. Sift in the flour, cream of tartar, baking powder, 1 teaspoon of the cinnamon, the nutmeg, and salt and stir to combine.

Mix the remaining cinnamon and sugar in a small bowl and sprinkle onto a plate. Roll the dough into 18 to 22 walnut-sized balls, then roll them in the cinnamon sugar to coat. Place well spaced apart on the prepared cookie sheets and flatten slightly.

Bake in a preheated oven at 400°F for 12 to 15 minutes until firm. Let cool on the cookie sheets for 2 minutes, then transfer to wire racks to cool completely.

GINGERDEAD MEN

Are the neighbors up all night slicing and dicing corpses? Do you want to shut them up once and for all? Or perhaps you're having trouble stocking up on a decent harvest of corpses? Whatever your motives, these innocent-looking patties will bring down your victims quickly and cleanly. Save the spectacle of agonizing death throes and bloodcurdling screams for another occasion—these biscuits are meant for swift dispatch.

Sufficient.—for 12 to 14 Gingerdead Men

1 cup whole-wheat flour
1 cup all-purpose flour, sifted with
   1 teaspoon baking powder
2 teaspoons ground ginger
½ teaspoon ground cinnamon
pinch of ground cloves

¾ stick chilled unsalted butter,
   diced
½ cup soft light brown sugar
1 tablespoon molasses
2 tablespoons light corn syrup
1 small egg, lightly beaten
handful of dried currants, to decorate

Method.—Line 2 cookie sheets with nonstick parchment paper. Place the flours and spices in a bowl or food processor, add the butter, and rub in with the fingertips or process until the mixture resembles fine bread crumbs. Add the sugar, molasses, light corn syrup, and egg and mix or pulse until just combined.

Tip the mixture onto a floured surface and knead gently until smooth. Roll out to ⅛ inch in thickness, then cut into 12 to 14 large gingerdead man shapes, rerolling the trimmings if necessary. Place the gingerdead men on the prepared cookie sheets and press in dried currants for eyes.

Bake in a preheated oven at 350°F for 15 to 18 minutes until golden. Let cool on the cookie sheets for 2 to 3 minutes, then transfer to wire racks to cool completely.

GINGERDEAD MEN

*If you have the correct spells and incantations on hand then
you can of course bring these minions to life to do your evil bidding.*

TOENAIL MACAROONS

A classic canapé for monster soirées in yesteryear, toenails were traditionally collected from the gnarly feet of the most unsanitary humans to ensure maximum crunchiness. Advancements in personal hygiene led to a global toenail shortage so the recipe has been adapted to include almonds. Although not authentic, you're less likely to suffer crippling stomach cramps after eating this version.

Sufficient.—for about 15 macaroons

2 egg whites
½ cup superfine sugar
1 cup ground almonds
blanched almonds, to decorate

Method.—Line a large cookie sheet with nonstick parchment paper. Beat the egg whites in a clean bowl with a hand-held electric mixer until peaking. Gradually beat in the sugar, a spoonful at a time, until thick and glossy. Add the ground almonds and stir in until combined.

Drop about 15 dessertspoonfuls of the mixture, slightly apart, onto the prepared cookie sheet, then press an almond on top of each.

Bake in a preheated oven at 350°F for about 15 minutes until the macaroons are pale golden and just crisp. Let cool on the cookie sheet for 5 minutes, then transfer to a wire rack to cool completely.

TOENAIL MACAROONS

Fresh toenails can prove difficult to extract; if you are using them,
leave your human in a cage or dungeon for several months until fungus sets in.

Common Ailments &
Recommended Cures

Members of the community suffer from a number of ailments that can be successfully treated and cured with a range of simple potions, ointments, and possets. If you have the raw ingredients, treatments are usually fairly straightforward to prepare and it's worth keeping a few multi-use medications in the house for overnight or dinner guests. Bear in mind the size of the patient—Giants will generally need about four times the dose of a Mummy or mechanical monster, while the excruciatingly slow metabolism of Zombies means they only require a half dose.

OPTIMISM

An extended bout of optimism can prove fatal or, when it progresses to enthusiasm, can develop into a lifelong condition. However, a quick response to the initial symptoms will mean the patient will suffer no more than a few acts of goodwill and some singing in the shower. Begin by administering a couple of heaped teaspoons of Salt Made from Tears of Anger. This can be added to food or taken with water. If symptoms don't improve within 24 hours, self-flagellation should quickly reinstate an aura of doom and gloom.

FEAR OF HEIGHTS

This can be a debilitating condition for members of city-rampaging communities such as Mothra, King Kong, and Godzilla, as well as airborne individuals such as Vampire Bats. It tends to lie undetected until it is activated by a combination of extreme altitude and an adverse reaction to sweetmeats. It can usually be cured instantly by reciting a simple incantation—*Ibus Ibus Imperious* works for Vampire Bats, while *Forte et Fidele* should be repeated for oversized patients.

FANGIVITIS

Gum disease is particularly rampant among those with a penchant for more rancid human parts—brains, gore, viscera, and entrails to name but a few. Gums can swell and sufferers will experience fang-ache and bleeding after prolonged organ meat banquets. A thorough clean with Fang Floss will dislodge fermenting foodstuffs, while a good swill of minty monster wash will disinfect the gums.

FUR LICE

This is a common complaint among long-haired and fur-endowed individuals and, in the past, the constant itching almost drove some remote Yeti tribes to the brink of extinction. These days, the proximity to apothecaries means the condition can usually be cured in a couple of days. An unguent of rat spittle, ground femur, and rotting geriatric flesh should be smeared on the fur and left overnight.

INGROWN CLAW

As well as being extremely painful, this can put a dampener on the nocturnal hunting practices of many communities, namely Werewolves, Trolls, and Ogres. The cure is a simple procedure to perform for individuals with digits—simply pull the claw out of the skin and trim it back with a set of trimming shears (use an angle grinder for larger patients).

1,000-YEAR CURSE COOKIES

When you've exhausted frights, scares, and the evil eye, it's time to resort to a good old-fashioned curse. The combination of ingredients has been crafted to provide an exact measure of 1,000 years of misery per cookie, if you repeat the name of the recipient when stirring the mixture. Humans should stir less, as their inferior life expectancy means 1,000 years would be wasted on mortal victims.

Sufficient.—for 16 cookies

1 stick unsalted butter, softened
1 cup soft light brown sugar
1 teaspoon vanilla extract
1 egg, lightly beaten
1 tablespoon milk
1½ cups all-purpose flour
1 teaspoon baking powder
1½ cups semisweet chocolate chips

Method.—Line a large cookie sheet with nonstick parchment paper. Beat together the butter and sugar in a large bowl until pale and fluffy. Mix in the vanilla extract, then gradually beat in the egg, beating well after each addition. Stir in the milk. Sift in the flour and baking powder, then fold in. Stir in the chocolate chips.

Drop about 16 level tablespoons of the mixture, about 1½ inches apart, onto the prepared cookie sheet, then lightly press with a floured fork.

Bake in a preheated oven at 350°F for 15 minutes or until lightly golden. Transfer to a wire rack to cool.

1,000-YEAR CURSE-REVERSE COOKIES

If you regret dishing out a 1,000-year curse during a fit of fury, you can reverse the effects by baking a batch of these cookies and stirring in a counterclockwise direction. They'll work for up to one week after the curse was ingested so it's worth having the ingredients in stock just in case. If not reversing a curse, they will imbue the eater with an unexpected run of good luck.

Sufficient.—for about 20 cookies

½ stick slightly salted butter, softened,
   plus extra for greasing
¾ cup light brown sugar
1 egg, lightly beaten
1 cup all-purpose flour sifted with
   1 teaspoon baking powder
1 cup white chocolate chips or 5 oz white
   chocolate, chopped

Method.—Beat together the butter and sugar in a bowl until combined. Beat in the egg until smooth and creamy. Add the flour and chocolate and mix to a paste.

Roll heaped teaspoonfuls of the mixture into about 20 balls and place spaced well apart on 2 greased cookie sheets.

Bake in a preheated oven at 350°F for about 15 minutes or until the cookies have spread and are pale golden. Let firm up on the cookie sheets for 2 minutes, then transfer to a wire rack to cool completely.

BUMP-IN-THE-NIGHT BISCUITS

Everyone assumes that monsters are genetically programmed to go "bump in the night." In reality, we all know that it takes years of extracurricular classes and daily practice to perfect the skill. These biscuits will help those of you struggling to pass your "Quiet Entrance" and "Art of Surprise" exams, or nocturnal humans with a malevolent streak.

Sufficient.—for 10 to 12 biscuits

2 cups all-purpose flour, sifted with
   3½ teaspoons baking powder
1 teaspoon ground cinnamon
½ teaspoon ground ginger
1 stick unsalted butter, softened
½ cup demerara (raw) sugar,
   plus extra for sprinkling (optional)

1 teaspoon grated orange zest
¾ cup golden raisins
½ cup dried currants
2 oz candied peel or chopped
   candied cherries
1 large egg, lightly beaten
3 to 4 tablespoons milk

Method.—Line a large cookie sheet with nonstick parchment paper. Sift the flour, baking powder, and spices into a large bowl. Add the butter and rub in with the fingertips until the mixture resembles fine bread crumbs, then stir in the sugar, orange zest, golden raisins, dried currants, and mixed peel or cherries. Pour in the egg and add enough of the milk to form a soft, slightly sticky dough.

Drop 10 to 12 mounds of the mixture onto the prepared cookie sheet so that they resemble rocks and sprinkle with a little extra sugar, if using.

Bake in a preheated oven at 400°F for 18 to 20 minutes until golden. Transfer to a wire rack to cool slightly, then serve warm.

BUMP-IN-THE-NIGHT BISCUITS

Creates the weightiest of bumps,
guaranteed to frighten humans of all ages.

WEREWOLF BISCUITS

Not every Werewolf wants to unleash its inner beast during a full moon—it's sometimes downright inconvenient. If you want to help a friend take control of their transformations, give them one of these biscuits on the evening of a full moon. It might take a few attempts to get the dose right so, if they still notice some sprouting of body hair and the urge to howl, they should eat two biscuits next time.

Sufficient.—for 8 biscuits

2 cups all-purpose flour, plus extra
    for dusting
1 cup rice flour or ground rice
½ cup superfine sugar, plus extra
    for dusting
pinch of salt
2 sticks unsalted butter, softened,
    plus extra for greasing

Method.—Sift the flours (or flour and ground rice), sugar, and salt into a bowl, add the butter, and rub in with the fingertips. When the mixture starts to bind, gather it with one hand into a ball. Knead on a lightly floured surface to a soft, smooth, pliable dough.

Put the dough in a 8-inch pie pan set on a greased cookie sheet. Press it out with your knuckles to fit the pan. Mark the dough into 8 pieces using the back of a knife. Prick right through to the cookie sheet with a fork in a neat pattern. Cover and chill for at least 1 hour before baking, to firm it up.

Bake in a preheated oven at 300°F for 45 to 60 minutes or until pale-biscuit-colored but still soft. Let cool and shrink before removing the ring, then dust lightly with superfine sugar. When cold, cut into 8 biscuits.

GRRRRR WOOF AWHOOOO HOWL

Note: this recipe has been translated for use by Werewolves

Sniiiif YAAAAAAAAp grrrrr, grrrrr grr sniff?? Grr grr grr! Awhoooo grr wooooood AROOOOOooo a grrrr gr wooooooooof woooof gr wooooof. BAAAAAARK gr yaaaaaaap. Hoooooooooowl.

Grrr grrrf.—yap 12 grrr yap yap

13 oz AWOOOOOOO ruff
   GRRRR
¾ cup HOOOOOWWWWWWLL
   grrrr grrrr!
3 awwwwww grrrrrrrr YAP
2 GRRRR Sniiiiiiffff sniiiffff
1 cup BARK! BARK! Awooo
½ to ¾ cup yaaaaap yap yap

Howl.—YAAAAAAP! Awwwww grrr grrr, grrrrr hoooooooooooowl. Awooooo GRRRR! BAAARK sniffff grrr BARRRRK! AWWWOoOOOOOooooOOOOOoo.
RAAAASP. Wooof. Grrr grrrr grr yap yap yap. GRRRRR! GRRRRR! Arooooo. Snniiiif, grrrr grrrr! Wooooof woof woof woof grrrrrrrr. BAARRk. AROOOooo. YAAAp yap yap yap yap yap yap.
AAAWWWWWOOOOOOOooooooooOOOOOOoooOoOOOOOOOOOoo!

UNDER-THE-BED BARS

Since that pesky Edison invented the light bulb, many Under-the-Bed and In-the-Cupboard Monsters have found themselves trapped under a bed or in a cupboard for hours, patiently waiting for the light to be switched off. Keep a couple of these hearty bars stashed in your scaring sack and you can bide your time without a giveaway stomach grumble.

Sufficient.—for 12 bars

1 cup whole-wheat flour
½ cup all-purpose flour, sifted with
   ½ teaspoon baking powder
1½ cups chilled slightly salted butter,
   diced, plus extra for greasing

½ teaspoon ground cinnamon
1¾ cups rolled oats
1 cup light brown sugar
1⅓ cups fresh blueberries
vanilla sugar, for sprinkling

Method.—Place the flours in a bowl or food processor, add the butter, and rub in with the fingertips or process until the mixture resembles bread crumbs. Add the cinnamon, oats, and light brown sugar and stir in or blend briefly until the mixture makes coarse crumbs and starts to cling together.

Tip about half the mixture into a greased 11 x 7 inch shallow baking pan and spread in an even layer. Pack down with the back of a spoon to make a firm base. Scatter with the blueberries and sprinkle with the remaining crumb mixture.

Bake in a preheated oven at 350°F for about 50 to 60 minutes until the crumbs on top are deep golden. Let stand to cool in the pan, then sprinkle with vanilla sugar and cut into 12 bars.

UNDER-THE-BED BARS

Four small bars will suffice for one night of scaring.
Pack with a thermos of corpse-infused coffee.

STRAWBERRY SHORTDEADS

The original version of these innocent-looking treats was given away when hunters needed help luring victims to their doom, or by humans wanting to dish out a doily-lined plate of revenge. The subtle poison was well hidden among the other ingredients and just one shortdead would have your victim eating out of the palm of your hand. Unfortunately, following a few incidences of mistaken identity, the biscuits were banned and this alternative recipe was swiftly introduced.

Sufficient.—for 12 shortdeads

1¾ cups all-purpose flour, plus extra
    for dusting
½ cup cornstarch
1½ sticks chilled slightly salted butter,
    diced, plus extra for greasing
¼ cup superfine sugar

Filling
1¼ cups sifted confectioners' sugar,
    plus extra for dusting
⅔ stick unsalted butter, softened
1 teaspoon vanilla extract
1 teaspoon boiling water
⅓ cup strawberry jam

Method.—Place the flours in a bowl or food processor, add the butter, and rub in with the fingertips or process until the mixture resembles coarse bread crumbs. Add the sugar and mix or blend to a dough. Seal in plastic wrap and chill for 1 hour.

Roll out the dough on a lightly floured surface to ¼ inch thick. Cut out disks using a 2-inch plain cookie cutter, rerolling the trimmings to make about 24. Place slightly apart on a large greased cookie sheet.

Bake in a preheated oven at 375°F for 15 minutes until very pale golden. Transfer to a wire rack to cool.

Make the filling. Beat together the confectioners' sugar, butter, and vanilla extract in a bowl until smooth. Add the measured water and beat until pale and creamy. Sandwich the biscuits together in pairs using the buttercream and jam. Serve dusted with confectioners' sugar.

STRAWBERRY SHORTDEADS

Though utterly fatal to humans, these are in fact quite delicious treats for Swamp Creatures, Zombies, and most Giant Apes.

BURSTING BOIL BISCUITS

Boil lancing is a dying trade, which means fresh pus, scabs, and crusty skin are increasingly difficult to procure. If you don't have a human delicacy deli nearby, or budget is an issue, this alternative recipe uses more accessible ingredients but the results are still delicious.

Sufficient.—for about 24 biscuits

½ cup sweetened condensed milk
1 cup cornflakes
½ cup sliced almonds
2 tablespoons chopped candied cherries
¼ cup chopped pecans
¼ cup chopped macadamia nuts or
    2 tablespoons chopped unsalted peanuts

Method.—Line 2 x 12-hole nonstick mini muffin pans with paper mini muffin cups, or lightly grease or line 2 large cookie sheets with nonstick parchment paper.

Put the condensed milk in a saucepan over low heat and warm through, then remove from the heat and stir in the remaining ingredients.

Drop about 24 small spoonfuls of the mixture into the prepared mini muffin pans or onto the cookie sheets.

Bake in a preheated oven at 350°F for 10 to 12 minutes until golden. Let cool in the pans until hardened, then transfer to a wire rack to cool completely.

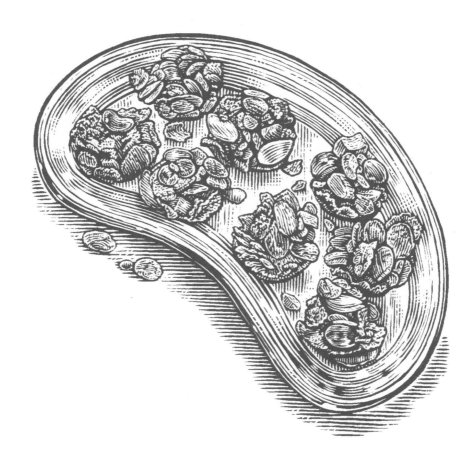

BURSTING BOIL BISCUITS

*Lancing a boil at the ideal moment for maximum pus yield is an art form,
and best performed by trained professionals.*

AAARRRRGGGHHHH-MARETTI BISCUITS

If you've let your scaring skills get a bit rusty lately, these sweet piquant bites will give you a boost in the "boo" department. They were traditionally served with a cup of toenail-infused tea to anyone who deserved a long night of extreme terror. Also good for human parents who want to teach their offspring that life isn't all princesses and happily ever afters.

Sufficient.—for about 30 biscuits

melted butter, for greasing
2 egg whites
1¾ cups ground almonds
1 cup superfine sugar
1 tablespoon Amaretto liqueur
2 tablespoons sifted confectioners' sugar,
     for dusting

Method.—Line 2 cookie sheets with parchment paper and brush with melted butter. Beat the egg whites in a clean bowl with a hand-held electric mixer until stiff peaks form. Fold in the almonds, superfine sugar, and Amaretto to form a stiff mixture.

Drop about 30 teaspoons of the mixture, at least ¾ inch apart, onto the prepared cookie sheets. Alternatively, roll teaspoons of the mixture into balls, then place on the cookie sheets and flatten slightly.

Bake in a preheated oven at 325°F for 15 minutes until light golden and firm at the edges. Let cool on the cookie sheets for 5 minutes, then transfer to a wire rack to cool completely, and serve dusted with the confectioners' sugar.

ANZAC BISCUITS

In the halcyon days of hunting, home cooks would try and source genuine Australians or New Zealanders for these antipodean munchies: the overexposure to sunlight and a happy disposition made for tender flesh. But expensive air fares and a Southern Hemisphere flight embargo on certain monster tribes made it increasingly difficult to obtain the raw ingredients, so a creative celebrity Cyclops came up with this mouth-watering alternative.

Sufficient.—for 28 to 30 biscuits

1 cup all-purpose flour
1 cup rolled oats
½ cup desiccated coconut
½ cup chopped ready-to-eat
   semi-dried figs

1 cup superfine sugar
1 stick unsalted butter
2 tablespoons light corn syrup
1 teaspoon baking soda
1 tablespoon boiling water

Method.—Line 2 large cookie sheets with nonstick parchment paper. Mix together the flour, oats, coconut, figs, and sugar in a large bowl.

Put the butter and light corn syrup in a small saucepan over low heat and warm until just melted. Put the baking soda in a small bowl and stir in the boiling water. Add to the melted butter, then stir into the dry ingredients.

Use lightly floured hands to roll the mixture into 28 to 30 walnut-sized balls, then place on the prepared cookie sheets.

Bake in a preheated oven at 400°F for 10 to 12 minutes until golden. Transfer to wire racks to cool.

Seasonal Humans

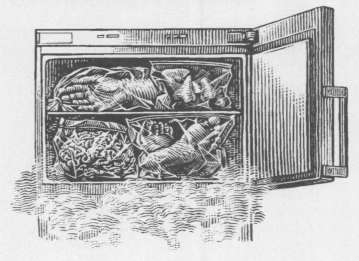

Although it is now possible to source virtually every type of human year-round, the quality is much improved if you shop seasonally. Discerning foodies know their imported Sarahs from their locally sourced ones so don't try and pull the fur over their eyes—stick to seasonal ingredients and adjust your meal plan to suit. Here's a guide to when the most common humans are at their best.

JANUARY–MARCH

Avoid pub-reared Europeans during the early months of the year, as they tend to be very pasty and have poor circulation. Antipodeans are at their best now and you should be able to place an order with your local dismemberer.

IN SEASON

Kylies, Lachlans, Corys, and Glorias are all at their prime. As they're already sun-ripened they don't need a lot of cooking—serve with a snot purée.

APRIL–JUNE

This is the time to shop for Americans, as the clement weather across many of the States results in low-stress meat with unclogged sweat glands. It's also a good time to shop for those from Japan and the Far East, though it's worth paying a little extra for free-range, smog-free varieties from outside of major cities.

IN SEASON

Paiges, Logans, Ellas, Brooklyns, Tysons, and Chelseas are the best-quality humans in this category. They freeze well so you can stock up on supplies for the whole year.

JULY–SEPTEMBER

Northern Europeans have been exposed to their annual rations of sunlight by now so they'll be at their prime. If you're lucky, you might find some sporty specimens with more muscle definition. Those from Southeast Asia can be slightly soggy at this time of year due to intense monsoons so are best avoided.

IN SEASON

Sarahs, Pauls, Helens, Davids, and Alis are the names to look out for. Sear the meat over a fire pit for a flame-grilled flavor and serve with a selection of salads.

OCTOBER–DECEMBER

Southern Europeans and hardy Canadians tend to taste best around this time of year but most humans should have a healthy paunch by December, as they string out their festive celebrations for a number of months.

IN SEASON

Liams, Williams, Chads, Olivias, Juans, and Lucias are all ready for the pot. Slow cooking suits these humans and you can add root vegetables and swamp herbs.

Hoxton Street Monster Supplies

ESTP 1818

~ Purveyor of Quality Goods for Monsters of Every Kind ~

CAKES
&
BAKES

INCLUDING
CLOTTED BLOOD CAKES
& FRESH MAGGOT BROWNIES

CLOTTED BLOOD CAKES

Those with nocturnal habits often need a mid-morning pick-me-up and blood was always the tipple of choice. However, the profusion of coffee shops has meant that many tribes have adopted the human predilection for caffeine, making fresh blood less popular. The traditional blood clots have been replaced in this recipe to appeal to modern tastes.

Sufficient.—for 20 cakes

7 oz white chocolate, broken into pieces
1 stick unsalted butter
3 eggs
1 cup superfine sugar
1 teaspoon vanilla extract
1 cup all-purpose flour
1 teaspoon baking powder
½ cup dried cranberries

Method.—Line a 7 x 11 x 2 inch baking pan with nonstick parchment paper and snip diagonally into the corners so that the paper fits snugly.

Melt half the chocolate and the butter in a heatproof bowl set over a saucepan of gently simmering water. Beat the eggs, sugar, and vanilla extract in a separate bowl with a hand-held electric mixer until light and frothy and the beater leaves a trail when lifted.

Fold the chocolate and butter mixture into the beaten eggs with a metal spoon. Sift the flour and baking powder over the top and then fold in gently. Chop the remaining chocolate and fold half of it into the mixture with half the cranberries.

Pour the mixture into the prepared pan and scatter with the remaining chocolate and cranberries. Bake in a preheated oven at 350°F for 30 to 35 minutes until well risen. Let cool in the pan.

Lift out of the pan, peel off the paper, and cut the cake into 20 squares.

CLOTTED BLOOD CAKES

Ideal for mid-morning snacking, these dainty cakes will satisfy your bloodlust without the risk of hitting a messy artery.

FRESH MAGGOT BROWNIES

This sweet treat was traditionally served at inter-tribal balls and graveyard gatherings. Fresh maggots were essential for the chewy consistency but quality varied greatly between suppliers, and even free-range maggots were affecting those with food intolerances. This allergy-friendly variation can be enjoyed by everyone.

Sufficient.—for 15 brownies

1 stick butter, plus extra for greasing
3 oz semisweet chocolate, broken
    into pieces
1½ cups soft light brown sugar
2 eggs, beaten

few drops of vanilla extract
½ cup ground almonds
3 tablespoons cornmeal or polenta
5 oz mixed nuts, toasted and
    coarsely chopped

Method.—Grease an 11 x 7 inch baking pan and line with nonstick parchment paper, snipping diagonally into the corners so that the paper fits snugly.

Melt the chocolate and butter in a heatproof bowl set over a saucepan of gently simmering water. Stir in all the remaining ingredients and combine well.

Pour the mixture into the prepared pan and bake in a preheated oven at 350°F for 30 minutes until slightly springy in the center. Let cool in the pan for 10 minutes, then cut into 15 squares.

FRESH MAGGOT BROWNIES

Graveyards are the perfect place to dig for maggots, if using;
they feast on the bounty of corpses there, giving them a pleasant humanlike taste.

BRAAAIIINNNN CAKE

Note: this recipe has been translated for use by Zombies

Urrrrgggghhhh. RAAAAAAAAAH. Ugggg. BRAAAAAINS. Oog. AAAAaaarrrr oooooooooog a aaaaaar ar uughhhhhhh. RAAAAH OOOOOOORG? BRAAAINS! Brrraaaaiinnnnss. Uuuugghhhh aaar errrrrrrrg.

ARRRR—uuuuurg ughh 8 Zombies

2 cups BRRRRAAAAAIIIIINNNN
¼ cup uuurrgh urgh errrr
3 oz errrrrrrggg?
1 teaspoon AAAAAARR ar ARRRR
¼ cup ooooo raaaaaahhh

Method.—OOoooog. BBBRRAAAAIIINNNNS! Brraaaaiiiinns. AAAR! Errrrrg aaaaaar aaar aaaarrr oooooooo urrghhhhhhhh RRAAAAHHHH brrrrainss a aar ooog. Reeeeeeeeeh aarr RAAAH oooooo. EERRRRG! ERRRRRGG!

OOOOOOGG. ERRRRRG. Aar uuuuurg. URGHH! Braaiiinns. BRRRAINS! AAARrrgghh. Gruuunt aaar OOOooOOOG. ARRRR RAAAH oooooouuuurrrghhh. Errrrg ughh uuugh. Brrrrains.

GGGRRRRRR. Uurrrg. Blleeuuurrrrggh. AArr arrrr aaarrr. BRAINS. Sluuuuuur grooog RAAAH URRRRGH.

MUCUS TARTS

Central heating and high-dose cold and flu remedies mean there's less good-quality human snot on the market these days. You can still find it in a handful of specialist shops in London, but it doesn't travel well. At a push, you can use animal snot but if you're not keen on the earthy aftertaste, try this snot-free alternative.

Sufficient.—for 12 tarts

1 tablespoon vanilla sugar	2 egg yolks
½ teaspoon ground cinnamon	2 tablespoons superfine sugar
14½ oz chilled sweet shortcrust pastry	1 teaspoon vanilla extract
a little flour, for dusting	1¼ cups heavy cream
3 eggs	¾ cup milk
	sifted confectioners' sugar, for dusting

Method.—Mix the vanilla sugar with the cinnamon. Cut the pastry in half and roll out each piece on a lightly floured surface to an 8-inch square. Sprinkle 1 square with the spiced sugar and position the second square on top. Reroll the pastry to a 16 x 12 inch rectangle and cut out 12 circles, each 4 inches across.

Press the pastry circles into the sections of a 12-hole nonstick muffin pan, pressing them firmly into the bottom and around the sides. Prick each pastry bottom with a fork, line with a square of foil, add ceramic baking beans, and bake in a preheated oven at 375°F for 10 minutes. Remove the foil and beans and bake for a further 5 minutes. Reduce the oven temperature to 325°F.

Beat together the eggs, egg yolks, superfine sugar, and vanilla extract in a heatproof bowl. Put the cream and milk into a saucepan and heat until bubbling around the edges. Pour it over the egg mixture, stirring. Strain into a pitcher and pour into the pastry crusts.

Bake for about 20 minutes or until the custard is only just set. Let cool in the pan, then remove and serve dusted with confectioners' sugar.

SPICED EARWAX PIE

Earwax has always been a kitchen cupboard staple for any self-respecting home cook and a pie was the perfect way to bake with it. The classic recipe was passed down the generations but modern life isn't conducive to waiting six months for earwax to fully mature. This super-quick wax-free version with no fermenting time was developed for those struggling with their work-life balance.

Sufficient.—for 8 monster servings of pie

2¾ cups light corn syrup
2 tablespoons butter
juice of 1 lemon
1½ cups fresh bread crumbs
2 oz candied ginger (or drained stem ginger in syrup), chopped
2 Braeburn apples, cored and grated
15 oz shortcrust pastry
milk, to glaze

Method.—Put the light corn syrup and butter in a saucepan and heat gently until melted. Stir in the lemon juice, bread crumbs, ginger, and apples, then let cool.

Roll out the pastry on a lightly floured surface until slightly larger than a greased 9½-inch loose-bottomed tart pan. Lift the pastry over a rolling pin, drape into the pan, then press over the bottom and up the sides. Trim off the excess pastry and reserve.

Pour the syrup mixture into the tart crust. Roll out the pastry trimmings, cut narrow strips, and arrange in a lattice. Use a little milk to stick the strips to the edges and brush the strips all over.

Place the tart on a preheated hot cookie sheet and bake in a preheated oven at 375°F for 40 to 50 minutes until golden and the filling has set. Check after 30 minutes and cover the top loosely with foil if the tart seems to be browning too quickly. Serve warm or cold.

SPICED EARWAX PIE

If time allows, fully matured earwax yields a warm, sticky pie like no other.

MASHED FAIRY CUPCAKES

These decadent cakes were traditionally saved for extra-special occasions, as edible fairies cost more per ounce than gold. For an impressive decorative flourish, chefs would shake the fairy wands over the finished cakes to scatter with glitter (ensuring the wands weren't cursed or the cakes tended to imbue a warm and cuddly feeling). This recipe isn't suitable for strict Fairytarians, but it does offer a suitably shimmery alternative.

Sufficient.—for 12 cupcakes

12 shop-bought strawberry cupcakes

Frosting
1½ sticks unsalted butter, softened
3 cups sifted strawberry-flavored
    confectioners' sugar, or confectioners'
    sugar mixed with 1 drop of red
    food coloring
1 to 2 teaspoons milk or water

To decorate
edible sprinkles
edible shimmer sugar or glitter

Method.—Make the frosting. Beat together the butter and confectioners' sugar in a large bowl until pale and creamy. Add enough milk or water to form a smooth paste.

Spoon the frosting into a pastry bag fitted with a star-shaped tip, then pipe swirls on top of the cupcakes.

Sprinkle the cupcakes with edible sprinkles and edible shimmer sugar or glitter (make sure the glitter is clearly marked as being safe to eat).

MASHED FAIRY CUPCAKES

Be sure to avoid contaminating your cupcakes with a fairy curse;
the warm, happy feelings they induce can take days to wear off.

ABOMINABLE SNOWBALLS

Energy drinks freeze in blizzards so these bite-sized balls are the perfect boost for Yetis and other cold-blooded tribes. They can also be used as ammunition in slingshots, but aim carefully—a miss means the snowball will become a tasty treat for your intended victim, rather than your victim becoming a tasty treat for you.

Sufficient.—for 12 snowballs

12 shop-bought vanilla or lemon cupcakes

1½ tablespoons shredded coconut

Frosting

8 oz cream cheese

½ stick unsalted butter, softened

1½ cups sifted confectioners' sugar

2 teaspoons finely grated lime zest, plus extra thin strips of rind to decorate (optional)

2 teaspoons lime juice

1½ tablespoons shredded coconut

Method.—Make the frosting. Place the cream cheese, butter, confectioners' sugar, and lime zest and juice in a large bowl and beat together with a hand-held electric mixer until very smooth. Then beat in the shredded coconut.

Spoon the frosting into a pastry bag fitted with a plain tip, then pipe a swirl on each cupcake.

Scatter the frosting with the remaining coconut and serve decorated with extra lime rind, if liked.

WELSHMAN CAKES

This recipe was created to use up leftover Welshmen after the prosperous harvest of AD 894. Supplies are now low again—though some monster markets stock the dried or pickled variety—so you can substitute other nationalities. Be aware that the flavor will alter accordingly so, if you're not keen on culinary surprises, use the recipe below, which offers a close resemblance to the original.

Sufficient.—for about 12 to 14 cakes

1¾ cups all-purpose flour, sifted with
    1¾ teaspoons baking powder, plus
    extra for dusting
½ teaspoon mixed spice (optional)
pinch of salt
1 stick chilled butter, diced,
    plus extra for frying

½ cup superfine sugar,
    plus extra for sprinkling
¼ cup dried currants
1 egg, lightly beaten
1 to 2 tablespoons milk

Method.—Place the flour and baking powder mixture, mixed spice, if using, and salt in a large bowl. Add the butter and rub in with the fingertips until the mixture resembles coarse bread crumbs. Stir in the sugar and dried currants. Add the egg and mix together to form a firm dough, adding some of the milk if the dough feels dry.

Roll out the dough on a lightly floured surface to about ¼ inch thick. Cut out disks using a 3-inch fluted cookie cutter, rerolling the trimmings to make 12 to 14.

Heat a ridged grill pan or heavy skillet over medium heat until hot. Add a walnut-sized lump of butter and swirl it around until melted, then add the cakes, in batches, and cook for 4 to 5 minutes on each side or until golden brown and slightly risen. Repeat with the remaining cakes, adding a little more butter to the pan for each batch.

Sprinkle with extra superfine sugar and serve warm or cold.

WARM KIDNEY CUPCAKES

The original recipe stipulated freshly harvested kidneys, as they tend to toughen and dry out very quickly. Binge drinking among humans has resulted in a dramatic drop in the number and quality of organs available—if you're having problems sourcing them, this variation should still satiate a sweet tooth, if not a blood thirst.

Sufficient.—for 12 cupcakes

1 cup all-purpose flour, sifted with
  1 teaspoon baking powder
2 tablespoons cocoa powder
½ teaspoon baking soda
½ cup buttermilk
1 teaspoon vinegar
½ stick slightly salted butter, softened
½ cup superfine sugar

1 egg, lightly beaten
2 oz raw beets, peeled and finely grated
12 fresh cherries, to decorate

Frosting
7 oz cream cheese
2 teaspoons vanilla extract
3 cups sifted confectioners' sugar

Method.—Line a 12-hole muffin pan with paper muffin cups. Combine the sifted flour and baking powder mixture, cocoa powder, and baking soda in a bowl. Mix together the buttermilk and vinegar in a pitcher.

Beat together the butter and superfine sugar in a separate bowl until pale and creamy, then beat in the egg and grated beets. Sift half the flour mixture into the bowl and stir in gently with a large metal spoon. Stir in half the buttermilk mixture. Sift and stir in the remaining flour mixture, then add the remaining buttermilk mixture.

Divide the cake mixture between the paper cups. Bake in a preheated oven at 350°F for 20 to 25 minutes or until risen and just firm to the touch. Transfer to a wire rack and let cool.

Make the frosting. Beat the cream cheese until softened. Beat in the vanilla extract and confectioners' sugar until smooth. Swirl onto the cakes and top each one with a cherry to finish.

WARM KIDNEY CUPCAKES

*It is recommended to avoid using the kidneys of inebriated humans
as they give off an overwhelming taste of poor decisions and regret.*

NIGHT TERROR TORTE

Humans have begun to wise up to nightmares. Horror movies, although highly inaccurate, have succeeded in making them largely immune to monster fright tactics. If you've lost some of your people-scaring pizzazz, smuggle a slice of this onto the dessert trolley. Your victims' screams of terror will give you a new lease of fright.

Sufficient.—for 8 monster servings of torte

1 cup superfine sugar	1 stick butter, softened
¼ cup water	1 cup ground almonds
2 oranges, thinly sliced	2 eggs, lightly beaten
15 oz sweet shortcrust pastry	3½ oz semisweet chocolate, melted

Method.—Put half the sugar and the measured water in a saucepan and heat gently until the sugar has dissolved. Add the orange slices and cook over low heat for 30 minutes until the oranges are tender and most of the syrup has evaporated. Let cool.

Roll out the pastry on a lightly floured surface until a little larger than a greased 9½-inch fluted loose-bottomed tart pan. Lift the pastry over a rolling pin, drape into the pan, then press over the bottom and up the insides. Trim off the excess pastry so it stands a little above the top of the pan. Prick the bottom with a fork and let chill for 15 minutes.

Line the tart with nonstick parchment paper, add ceramic baking beans, and place on a cookie sheet. Bake in a preheated oven at 375°F for 10 minutes. Remove the paper and beans and bake for a further 5 minutes until pale golden and crisp. Reduce the oven temperature to 350°F.

Beat together the butter and the remaining sugar in a bowl until light and fluffy. Add the ground almonds, then gradually beat in the eggs until smooth. Set aside. Reserve 10 of the best orange slices, then drain and chop the rest. Stir the chocolate into the almond mixture, then mix in the chopped oranges. Spread into the torte crust, arrange the reserved orange slices on top, and bake for 30 minutes. Let cool for 30 minutes before removing from the pan.

NIGHT TERROR TORTE

Be sure to think truly appalling thoughts as you make this torte—
you will find that the screams of your victims will have an extra edge of misery if you do.

FRESH PUS PIE

Pus Pie was a firm favorite on the menu of many cadaver cafes up until about a century ago. It was delicious served warm and oozing from the oven or fire pit. The best pus was extracted from diseased humans and it could be very rich so diners were advised to limit themselves to one small slice. A dramatic drop in human diseases that produced oozing boils led to its demise and this modern recipe took over in popularity.

Sufficient.—for 8 monster servings of pie

13 oz sweet shortcrust pastry
a little flour, for dusting
1 cup superfine sugar
1 cup fresh lime juice
8 fresh lime leaves or the grated
    zest of 3 limes

3 eggs and 2 egg yolks
1½ sticks unsalted butter, at room
    temperature, plus extra for greasing
sifted confectioners' sugar, for dusting

Method.—Roll out the pastry on a lightly floured surface until a little larger than a greased 9-inch fluted loose-bottomed tart pan. Lift the pastry over a rolling pin, drape into the pan, then press over the bottom and up the insides. Trim off the excess pastry so it stands a little above the top of the pan. Prick the bottom with a fork. Let chill for 30 minutes.

Line the tart with nonstick parchment paper, add ceramic baking beans, and bake in a preheated oven at 400°F for 15 minutes. Remove the paper and beans and bake for a further 12 to 15 minutes until the pastry is crisp and golden. Let cool.

Put the sugar, lime juice, and lime leaves or lime zest in a saucepan. Heat gently until the sugar has dissolved. Bring to a boil and simmer for 5 minutes. Let cool for 5 minutes, then strain into a clean pan.

Stir in the eggs, egg yolks, and half the butter and heat gently, stirring, for 1 minute or until the sauce coats the back of the spoon. Add the remaining butter and whisk constantly until the mixture thickens.

Transfer the lime mixture to the tart crust and bake for 6 to 8 minutes until set. Let cool slightly, then serve warm, dusted with confectioners' sugar.

FRESH PUS PIE

Though the monster community fervently awaits the arrival of a plague or epidemic, advances in human medicine have sadly affected the availability of high-quality pus.

BATTERY ACID BRÛLÉE

Battery acid used to be the classic kick-starter for anyone created in a lab or with a penchant for mechanical snacks. One or two of these delicious desserts would be served to lackluster individuals as an energy booster, and to lubricate stiff or rusty joints. However, the caustic aftertaste often resulted in reflux so this less abrasive version of the recipe came into favor.

Sufficient.—for 6 brûlées

1 vanilla bean, split in half lengthwise
2½ cups heavy cream
8 egg yolks
¼ cup superfine sugar
3 tablespoons confectioners' sugar

Method.—Place the vanilla bean in a saucepan, pour in the cream, and bring almost to a boil. Remove from the heat and let stand for 15 minutes. Lift the bean out of the cream and, holding it against the side of the saucepan, scrape the seeds into the cream. Discard the rest of the bean.

Using a fork, mix together the egg yolks and superfine sugar in a heatproof bowl. Reheat the cream, then gradually mix it into the eggs and sugar. Strain the mixture back into the saucepan.

Place 6 ovenproof ramekins in a roasting pan, then divide the custard between them. Pour warm water around the dishes to come halfway up the sides, then bake in a preheated oven at 350°F for 20 to 25 minutes until the custard is just set with a slight softness at the center.

Let the dishes cool in the water, then lift them out and let chill in the refrigerator for 3 to 4 hours. About 25 minutes before serving, sprinkle with the confectioners' sugar and caramelize using a chef's torch (or under a hot broiler), then let stand at room temperature.

OFFICE-WORKER ROULADE

The temperature-controlled office results in soft, pulpy humans with a dulled fight-or-flight instinct. Ogres have been stocking up on this easy prey since the invention of commuting, with this roulade being a firm favorite after a successful raid. Remote working has affected stocks so we've created this vegetarian version for hard times.

Sufficient.—for 8 monster servings of roulade

4 egg whites

1¼ cups superfine sugar, plus extra
   for sprinkling

1 teaspoon cornstarch

1 teaspoon white wine vinegar

1 cup ready-to-eat dried apricots

1¼ cups water

¾ cup heavy cream

5 oz fromage blanc

Method.—Line a 13 x 9 inch jelly roll pan with nonstick parchment paper. Snip into the corners so the paper fits snugly and stands a little above the top of the sides.

Beat the egg whites in a large clean bowl until stiff peaks form. Gradually beat in the sugar, a spoonful at a time, until the mixture is thick and glossy. Mix the cornstarch and vinegar together until smooth, then fold into the meringue mixture.

Spoon the mixture into the prepared pan and level it off. Bake in a preheated oven at 375°F for 10 minutes until biscuit-colored and well risen. Reduce the heat to 325°F, and bake for a further 5 minutes until just firm to the touch and the top is slightly cracked.

Cover a clean dish cloth with nonstick parchment paper and sprinkle with sugar. Invert the hot meringue out onto the paper. Let cool for 1 to 2 hours.

Simmer the apricots in the measured water for 10 minutes until tender. Let cool, then purée until smooth.

Peel the paper off the meringue and spread with the purée. Whip the cream until it forms soft swirls, fold in the fromage blanc, then spoon over the purée. Starting from a short side, roll up the meringue to make a log shape. Place on a serving plate and slice.

CLOTTED BLOOD POUCHES

Note: this recipe has been translated for use by Vampire Bats

This recipe has been used for thousands of years by both Vampire Bats and Vampires themselves as a delightful way to sweeten up a blood harvest. The freshest blood was required in the original dish, as it would be served by polite society for cave warmings and belfry bops. This variation is ideal for non-Vampires, or bats with fang decay.

Sufficient.—for 22 to 24 pouches

1¼ sticks unsalted butter, softened
⅜ cup superfine sugar
1 large egg, lightly beaten
¾ cup ground almonds
2 cups all-purpose flour
about ¼ cup good-quality jam,
    such as raspberry or blackcurrant
sifted confectioners' sugar, for dusting

Method.—Line 2 large cookie sheets with nonstick parchment paper. Beat together the butter and sugar in a bowl until light and fluffy. Add the egg and ground almonds and beat well. Add the flour and mix to form a soft dough.

Roll the dough into 22 to 24 walnut-sized balls, then place on the prepared cookie sheets and flatten gently. Use your fingertip or a wooden spoon handle to create dips in the dough. Fill each one with one teaspoon of the jam, using a mixture of flavors, if liked. Bake in a preheated oven at 400°F for 12 minutes or until lightly golden. Let cool slightly on the cookie sheets, then transfer to wire racks to cool completely. Serve dusted with confectioners' sugar.

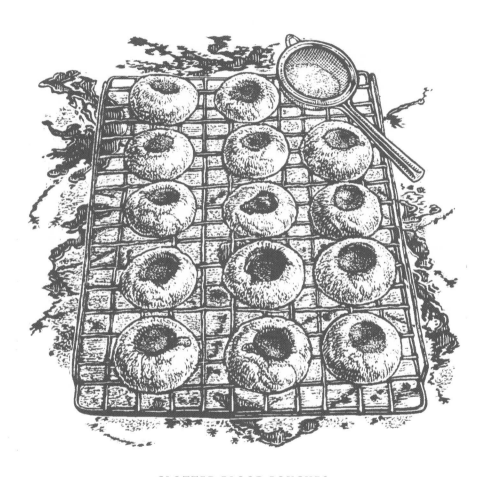

CLOTTED BLOOD POUCHES

When hanging upside-down,
take care not to allow your blood (or jam) to drip onto the floor.

CLASSIC KRAKEN CRISP

This recipe traditionally used captured sailors and was passed down the Kraken generations. Its popularity waned with the demise of nautical trade and pirating but has been adopted by other tribes who simply substitute landlubbers for the filling. Alternatively, you can bake this fruity version when the pantry is low on human stock.

Sufficient.—for 4 monster servings of crisp

10 plums, pitted and sliced
4 teaspoons superfine sugar
juice of 1 orange
1 stick butter
1 cup all-purpose flour
1 teaspoon ground cinnamon
¼ cup packed soft brown sugar
½ cup chopped hazelnuts

Method.—Put the plums, superfine sugar, and orange juice in a saucepan and cook for 3 minutes or until starting to soften, then spoon into an baking dish.

Melt the butter and mix together with the remaining ingredients. Crumble the mixture over the plums, breaking up any large clumps.

Bake in a preheated oven at 375°F for 20 to 25 minutes until the topping is crisp. Serve with plenty of custard or runny cow's turd.

TOENAIL-DUSTED SWEET CAKES

In the past, nose-to-tail-end hunters would source and dismember whole humans—and Toenail Cakes were a great way to use up every last scrap. A full set of fungus-infested toenails was considered a real treat and the original recipe introduced them to the dessert menu. Most tribes now buy prepackaged joints and cuts, so this updated recipe is for those who don't have easy access to truly disgusting toenails.

Sufficient.—for 24 cakes

1 stick unsalted butter, softened,
   plus extra for greasing
½ cup superfine sugar
2 eggs, lightly beaten
2 cups all-purpose flour, sifted
   with 2 teaspoons baking powder
pinch of salt
¼ cup milk
1 teaspoon vanilla extract

Coating
4 cups sifted confectioners' sugar
1¼ cups cocoa powder
½ to ¾ cup boiling water
2¼ cups desiccated coconut

Method.—Grease a 7 x 10 inch cake pan and line the bottom with parchment paper.

Beat together the butter and superfine sugar in a bowl until light and fluffy. Gradually incorporate the eggs, adding a little flour to prevent the mixture from curdling. Add the flour and salt and fold in with the milk and vanilla extract. Pour into the prepared pan and level the surface.

Bake in a preheated oven at 375°F for 25 to 30 minutes until risen and firm to the touch. Let cool in the pan for 5 minutes, then transfer to a wire rack and peel off the lining paper. Let stand overnight, then cut into 24 squares.

Sift the confectioners' sugar and cocoa powder into a bowl. Make a well in the center and beat in enough of the boiling water to form a smooth icing with a pouring consistency. Dip the top of each cake into the icing and then coat with the coconut. Let stand to set before serving.

Labels for Gifts

The tradition of gift-giving is an age-old custom that was originally part of tribal reconciliation in the ancient world. Today, different communities favor different occasions. For example, the undead are very unlikely to exchange presents on birthdays, but will happily splash out on expensive gifts on Day of the Undead. It is customary to include a personalized note with each gift so, if you're not endowed with a wicked wit or a romantic soul, we've prepared a few examples below that could be used for a number of occasions.

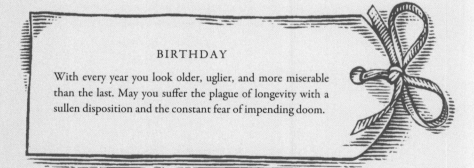

BIRTHDAY

With every year you look older, uglier, and more miserable than the last. May you suffer the plague of longevity with a sullen disposition and the constant fear of impending doom.

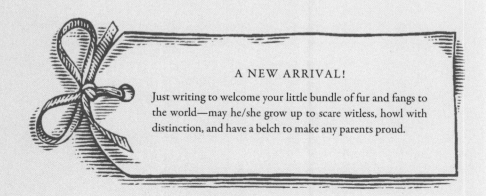

A NEW ARRIVAL!

Just writing to welcome your little bundle of fur and fangs to the world—may he/she grow up to scare witless, howl with distinction, and have a belch to make any parents proud.

GET WELL SOMETIME

I've heard you're not feeling well. What great news! I hope that you remain in the throes of agony for a long time to come, flailing in sweat-drenched fevers and taking advantage of some downtime from scaring and hunting humankind.

WEDDING ANNIVERSARY

I've put up with your flatulence, tendency to hog the bed, and mixed success with human cuts over the fire pit for 150 years. I'm looking forward to growing old with you disgracefully, as our fur thins and our fangs fall out.

THANK YOU

Here's a bunch of dead flowers to show my appreciation for the gut-churning meal you prepared on Saturday. The entrails were divine, the Pus Pie pastry was baked to perfection, and the free-range human torso was exquisitely rancid. Delicious!

Hoxton Street Monster Supplies

EST.D 1818

~ Purveyor of Quality Goods for Monsters of Every Kind ~

JAMS
&
PRESERVES

INCLUDING
OLDE-FASHIONED BRAIN JAM
& THICKEST HUMAN SNOT CURD

OLDE-FASHIONED BRAIN JAM

If you wanted to make the classic version of this recipe you had to source the stupidest humans—clever varieties had very bitter-tasting brains. Unfortunately, further education in modern times drastically reduced the availability of dim-witted people and the price of brains skyrocketed until the original recipe became too unaffordable to make. This updated version omits the brains but is no less delicious as a result.

Sufficient.—for 6 jars

1 small marrow squash, about 1½ to 1¾ lb, peeled, halved, seeded, and diced	½ lb blackberries
	1¼ cups water
3 lb just-ripe plums, quartered and pitted	3 lb granulated sugar, warmed
	1 tablespoon butter (optional)

Method.—Put the marrow squash, plums, blackberries, and measured water in a preserving pan, cover, and cook for 20 minutes until the fruits are just tender.

Pour the sugar into the pan and heat gently, stirring from time to time, until the sugar has dissolved. Bring to a boil, then boil rapidly until setting point (*see* page 157) is reached (15 to 20 minutes). Skim with a slotted spoon or stir in the butter to disperse the scum, if needed.

Ladle the jam into the warm, dry sterilized jars (*see* page 157), filling to the very top. Cover with screwtop lids, or with wax disks and cellophane tops secured with elastic bands. Label and let cool.

To serve, this jam is delicious simply eaten with bread and butter.

OLDE-FASHIONED BRAIN JAM

Spread thickly on wholebrain bread for a delicious treat.

THICKEST HUMAN SNOT CURD

Trolls, Ogres, and other human-hunters used to stock up on snot during flu season in order to enjoy this glutinous curd all year round. Human snot was a popular treat so this would also be appreciated as a gift by friends or neighbors who didn't own a snot extractor, or who lived in warmer climates where a lack of winter ills meant it was harder to procure. As snot became less readily available, Troll housewives developed this tasty alternative.

Sufficient.—for 3 assorted jars

1½ lb cooking apples, quartered, cored, peeled, and diced
½ cup ginger wine
grated zest and juice of 1 lemon
1 stick butter, diced

1¾ cups superfine sugar
3 eggs, beaten
2 oz drained stem ginger in syrup, finely chopped

Method.—Put the apples, ginger wine, and lemon zest and juice in a saucepan, cover, and cook gently for about 15 minutes, stirring from time to time, until the apples are soft. Let cool for 10 to 15 minutes.

Purée the apple mixture in a food processor or blender or press through a sieve. Place the butter in a large heatproof bowl set over a saucepan of simmering water and warm until just melted.

Add the sugar and apple purée to the bowl, then strain in the eggs and cook over medium heat for 40 to 50 minutes, stirring frequently until the sugar has dissolved and the eggs have thickened the mixture (take care not to have the heat too high or the eggs will curdle).

Stir in the chopped ginger, then ladle into warm, dry sterilized jars, filling to the very top. Cover with screwtop lids, or with wax disks and cellophane tops secured with elastic bands. Label and let cool. Store in the refrigerator for up to 2 weeks.

THICKEST HUMAN SNOT CURD

If you are struggling to procure the required amount of snot for a traditional recipe,
our Hoxton Street shop is stocked all year round.

BOILED BILE JAM

Under-the-Bed Monsters traditionally took a spoonful or two of Bile Jam before a scaring frenzy—the bile reacted with saliva to produce the most rancid breath imaginable. One exhalation used to render humans comatose, so this was ideal if you weren't as agile as you used to be. However, it proved almost fatal when taken accidentally on date nights—many a prospective romance was doomed—so it was removed from the menu and this alternative introduced.

Sufficient.—for 5 jars

4 lb ripe mangoes (about
 3 large ones)
grated zest and juice of 3 large limes

½ cup water
2 lb granulated sugar, warmed
3 passion fruits, halved

Method.—Cut a thick slice off either side of each mango to reveal the large, flattish seed. Trim the flesh from around the seed, then cut away the peel, dice the flesh, and place in a preserving pan. Cut criss-cross lines over the remaining mango slices, then press the skin side so that the squares of mango stand proud of the skin, like a hedgehog. Slide a knife under the cubes of mango to release, then add to the pan with the lime juice and measured water.

Cook, uncovered, over low heat for 8 to 10 minutes, stirring from time to time, until the mango is soft.

Add the lime zest and sugar and heat gently, stirring from time to time, until the sugar has completely dissolved. Bring to a boil, then let it boil rapidly until setting point is reached (10 to 20 minutes).

Turn off the heat, scoop the passion fruit seeds from the fruit with a teaspoon, and stir into the jam. Let cool for 5 to 10 minutes so the seeds will not rise in the jam, then spoon into warm, dry sterilized jars, filling to the very top. Cover with screwtop lids, or with wax disks and cellophane tops secured with elastic bands. Label and let cool.

BOILED BILE JAM

Served on top of a bowl of organ-meat yogurt, this makes for a delicious date-night dessert.

GUTS AND GARLIC CHUTNEY

Not one for Vampires and Vampire Bats but everyone else used to love the 16th-century recipe with its combination of fresh, warm guts and strong garlic. The beginning of the 18th century heralded a sharp rise in anaphylactic shock linked to gut consumption so the original recipe was lost to the annals of history and this light alternative was introduced.

Sufficient.—for 3 jars

1 garlic bulb (about 12 cloves),
    peeled and minced
10 oz onions, chopped
1 lb tomatoes, skinned (optional)
    and coarsely chopped
1 lb zucchini, diced
6 bell peppers of different colors,
    halved, seeded, and cut into strips

1 cup red wine vinegar
1¼ cups granulated sugar
1 tablespoon tomato paste
3 rosemary stems, leaves torn
    from stems and chopped
salt and pepper

Method.—Put all the ingredients in a preserving pan and cook, uncovered, over very low heat for 1½ hours, stirring from time to time, but more frequently toward the end of cooking as the chutney thickens.

Ladle into warm, dry sterilized jars, filling to the very top and pressing down well. Disperse any air pockets with a skewer or small knife and cover with screwtop lids. Label and let stand to mature in a cool, dark place for at least 3 weeks.

CLASSIC ORPHAN MARMALADE

This was traditionally served on toast for a leisurely weekend brunch, along with a Gallstone and Bile Smoothie (*see* page 142). Purists would source the most miserable orphans but had to carefully check the provenance—some unscrupulous suppliers were caught passing off human offspring from happy homes as abandoned wretches. When it became clear that authenticity couldn't be guaranteed, The Monster Marketing Board insisted that the original recipe was substituted for the one below.

Sufficient.—for 5 to 6 jars

2 lb Seville or regular oranges
  (about 6)
2 quarts water
juice of 1 lemon

3½ lb granulated sugar, warmed
  warmed
1¼ cups paacked dark brown sugar,
  warmed
1 tablespoon butter (optional)

Method.—Cut each orange into 6 wedges, then thinly slice. Tie the orange seeds in a square of cheesecloth. Put the oranges and seeds in a preserving pan, pour over the measured water, and add the lemon juice. Bring slowly to a boil, then simmer gently, uncovered, for about 1½ hours until reduced by almost half.

Add the sugar and heat gently, stirring from time to time, until the sugar has dissolved. Bring to a boil, then let boil rapidly until setting point is reached (10 to 20 minutes).

Lift out the cheesecloth bag, squeezing well. Skim with a slotted spoon or stir in the butter to disperse the scum, if needed. Ladle into warm, dry sterilized jars, filling to the very top. Cover with screwtop lids, or with wax disks and cellophane tops secured with elastic bands. Label and let cool.

To serve, this marmalade goes beautifully with sliced walnut bread.

CHUNKY ORGAN CHUTNEY

Traditional organ chutney was a versatile dish that used to be served as a sandwich filler, or with a selection of crudités—bones, eyeballs, toenails, etc. It was prepared by inhabitants of colder climes as a winter kitchen-cupboard staple, so human parts could be enjoyed outside hunting season. With vegetarianism on the rise, this adaptation has proved a firm favorite.

Sufficient.—for 4 jars

2 lb diced pumpkin flesh
2 onions, finely chopped
1 large orange, finely chopped, including skin and pith
2½ cups white wine vinegar
¾ lb granulated sugar
1 cinnamon stick, halved

2-inch piece of fresh ginger root, peeled and finely chopped
1 teaspoon dried crushed red chiles
1 teaspoon salt
a little black pepper
½ cup walnut pieces

Method.—Put all the ingredients in a preserving pan, cover, and cook gently for 1 hour, stirring from time to time, until softened. Remove the lid and cook for 30 to 60 minutes, stirring more frequently toward the end of cooking as the chutney thickens.

Ladle into warm, dry sterilized jars, filling to the very top and pressing down well. Disperse any air pockets with a skewer or small knife and cover with screwtop lids. Label and let stand to mature in a cool, dark place for at least 3 weeks.

CHUNKY ORGAN CHUTNEY

CAUTION
Never, under any circumstances, offer this vegetarian alternative to a Troll.
They will see it as a gross insult and are liable to tear their host to pieces in anger.

GIANT'S BEANSTALK CHUTNEY

A Giant kingdom specialty, this recipe traditionally made use of leftover beanstalks once the human had been devoured. Now that humans are permanently glued to smartphones and computers, they're less inquisitive and fewer make the doomed trip up the beanstalk. This has forced many Giants to become vegan and take up yoga as a pastime, and the chutney recipe has been adapted accordingly.

Sufficient.—for 6 jars

2 lb Kentucky wonder beans, trimmed

3¾ cups distilled malt vinegar

1½ lb demerara (raw) sugar

1 lb onions, chopped

1½ tablespoons turmeric

1½ tablespoons mustard powder

3 tablespoons black mustard seeds

3 tablespoons cornstarch

1 teaspoon salt

a little black pepper

3 tablespoons water

Method.—Half-fill a preserving pan with water, bring to a boil, then add the Kentucky wonder beans. Return to a boil and cook for 3 minutes. Drain in a colander, refresh under cold running water, then drain again. Thinly slice the beans or coarsely chop in a food processor.

Add the vinegar and sugar to the drained preserving pan, then add the onions. Cover and bring to a boil, then reduce the heat and simmer for 10 minutes.

Mix the remaining dry ingredients together in a bowl, then stir in the measured water until smooth. Stir this into the vinegar mixture, then simmer, uncovered, for 10 minutes, stirring until smooth and thickened.

Stir the blanched beans into the vinegar mixture and cook gently for 10 minutes, stirring frequently until just tender. Ladle into warm, dry sterilized jars, pressing the beans down well in the vinegar mix. Disperse any air pockets with a skewer or small knife and cover with screwtop lids. Label and let stand to mature in a cool, dark place for at least 3 weeks.

SWEET & SPICY CHILDREN'S TONGUES

In centuries past, children's tongues were a tasty by-product of silencing measures during human raids. The combination of sweet and spicy ingredients turned them into a piquant snack that was served as an appetizer at festive banquets. These days, small humans have been conditioned to brush their teeth twice a day and their tongues are far less slimy and rancid, so this modern recipe might be more appealing.

Sufficient.—for 2 jars

1 lb whole red finger chiles
2 cups apple cider vinegar or
   white wine vinegar
¼ cup set honey
¼ cup light brown sugar
4 bay leaves

4 sprigs of thyme
4 garlic cloves, sliced
1-inch piece of fresh ginger root,
   peeled and finely chopped
1 teaspoon coriander seeds
1 teaspoon salt

Method.—Cook the chiles in a saucepan of boiling water for 2 to 3 minutes until just softened. Tip into a colander, refresh under cold running water, and drain well.

Pour the vinegar into the drained pan and add all the remaining ingredients. Heat gently until the sugar has dissolved, then cook over medium heat for 5 minutes.

Pack the chiles and herbs from the vinegar tightly into warm, dry sterilized jars, then pour over the hot vinegar mixture, making sure that the chiles are completely covered by the vinegar. Cover with screwtop lids, label, and let stand to mature in a cool, dark place for 3 to 4 weeks.

FEE FI FO FUM SPREAD

The centerpiece of every self-respecting Giant's buffet table—but equally adored by all tribes—this delicately flavored dessert was traditionally presented with aged toe cheese from soap-dodging humans. Dinner party doyens would also serve it as a dipping sauce with couch potato bones and geriatric fingernails to really impress their guests. Reduce the quantities for the non-Giant community.

Sufficient.—for 2 large jars

4 lb quinces, down rubbed off, rinsed, and cut into 1-inch cubes

2 quarts water

a little sunflower oil, for brushing the pan and the insides of the jars

3 to 3½ lb granulated sugar

1 tablespoon butter (optional)

Method.—Put the quinces and measured water in a large pan, cover, and bring to a boil, then reduce the heat and simmer for 1 hour until very soft.

Purée the quinces and their liquid in batches in a food processor or blender, then press through a sieve into a large bowl. Discard the seeds, skin, and cores. Weigh the purée. Wash and dry the pan and brush with sunflower oil. Pour the purée back into the pan, add 1 pound sugar for every 1 pound purée, and cook over low heat, stirring from time to time, until the sugar has dissolved.

Cook, uncovered, over medium heat for 45 to 60 minutes, stirring more frequently toward the end of cooking, until the mixture makes large bubbles, has darkened slightly, and is so thick that the wooden spoon leaves a line across the bottom of the pan when drawn through the mixture. Skim with a slotted spoon or stir in the butter to disperse the scum, if needed.

Ladle quickly into warm, dry, sterilized wide-necked jars (square if possible) with tight-fitting lids, the insides of which have been lightly brushed with sunflower oil, filling to the very top. Cover with screwtop lids, label, and let cool.

Loosen with a round-bladed knife, turn out, slice, and serve with bread and cheese.

FEE FI FO FUM SPREAD

Though traditionally made with the blood of an Englishman (their stiff upper lip made the perfect spout for easy drainage), this alternative will suffice in a pinch.

PICKLED EYEBALLS

Pickled eyeballs have always been an acquired taste but they used to be particularly popular with Swamp Creatures. The sharp flavor and slimy consistency made them ideal as a bar snack or as an addition to swamp stews and cadaver casseroles. When spectacles became a common addition to the human face some time during the 13th century, it was increasingly difficult to extract eyeballs without creating a disturbance and lazy hunters adopted this eyeball-free recipe.

Sufficient.—for 1 very large jar

1¼ lb small shallots
2 tablespoons salt
2 cups sherry vinegar
½ cup superfine sugar
1 cup light brown sugar (not packed)
2 garlic cloves, unpeeled

4 small bay leaves
4 sprigs of thyme
4 sprigs of rosemary
pinch of salt
½ teaspoon peppercorns,
    coarsely crushed

Method.—Trim a little off the tops and roots of the shallots, then put in a bowl and cover with boiling water. Let soak for 3 minutes, then pour off the water and re-cover with cold water. Lift the shallots out one at a time and peel off the brown skins. Drain and layer in a bowl with the salt. Let stand overnight.

Tip the shallots into a colander and drain off as much liquid as possible. Rinse under cold running water, drain, and dry with paper towels.

Put the vinegar, sugars, garlic cloves, half the herbs, a pinch of salt, and the peppercorns in a saucepan and heat gently, stirring from time to time, until the sugar has dissolved. Increase the heat to medium and simmer for 5 minutes. Let cool.

Pack the shallots tightly into a warm, dry sterilized large jar with the remaining herbs. Strain and pour the cold vinegar syrup over the shallots, making sure that the shallots are covered with the vinegar to the very top. Cover with screwtop lids. Label and let stand to mature in a cool, dark place for 3 to 4 weeks.

PICKLED EYEBALLS

Despite lacking the much loved "pop" of the eyeball variety,
this dish retains the sliminess of the original recipe.

Labels for Buffets

With such an array of allergies, intolerances, and dietary requirements to contend with, a dinner party these days can be a minefield of forbidden ingredients and unexpected reactions.

Many hosts choose to serve a buffet to avoid embarrassing *faux pas* and to offer guests a choice of food—whatever their diet.

However, it's worth preparing labels for any dishes that might contain allergenic ingredients (and for fad-following, new-age eaters). There's nothing like an episode of anaphylaxis brought on by a stray tendon to put a dampener on proceedings.

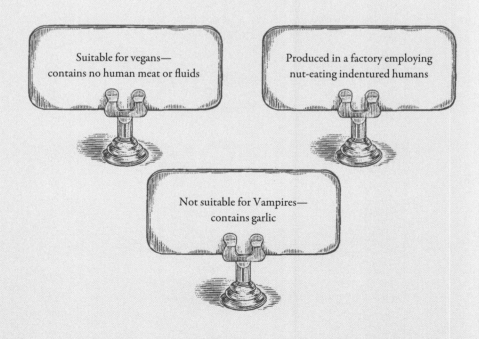

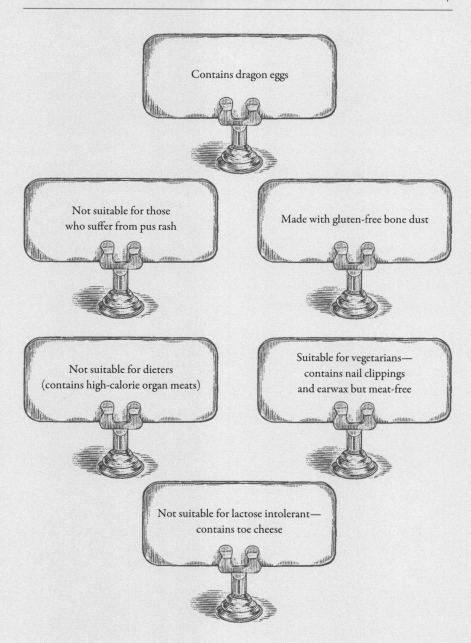

Contains dragon eggs

Not suitable for those who suffer from pus rash

Made with gluten-free bone dust

Not suitable for dieters (contains high-calorie organ meats)

Suitable for vegetarians— contains nail clippings and earwax but meat-free

Not suitable for lactose intolerant— contains toe cheese

Hoxton Street Monster Supplies

ESTD 1818

~ Purveyor of Quality Goods for Monsters of Every Kind ~

SAVORY SNACKS

for

ENTERTAINING MONSTERS

INCLUDING

UNICORN PIES

& CORPSE QUICHES

CHUNKY VOMIT DIP

Ogres traditionally prepared this foul-smelling delicacy as a dipping sauce for larger human roasts and pan-fried organs. However, its popularity spread and you can now find it in pop-up bodily fluid bars everywhere. Certain human ailments give the vomit a sickly sweet aftertaste so always source from those who are sick with terror, as opposed to illness. If unsure, this vegetable version of the dip will suffice in an emergency.

Sufficient.—for 6 monster servings of dip

3 ripe avocados
1 tomato, finely chopped
handful of cilantro leaves,
    finely chopped
½ teaspoon ground cumin
squeeze of lime juice
salt
tortilla chips, to serve

Method.—Halve and stone the avocados, then scoop the flesh out of the shells and place in a bowl.

Add the tomato, chopped cilantro, and cumin and coarsely mash together with a fork. Stir in the lime juice and season to taste with salt.

Serve immediately with tortilla chips or Crispy Skin (*see* page 113) for dipping.

CHUNKY VOMIT DIP

If your vomit is correctly sourced, the unmistakable tang of fear
brings this dip a delightful flavor.

CRISPY BAKED RIB BONES

The proliferation of processed snacks has led to monster offspring becoming lethargic and dull-witted over the last century. Crispy bones were quick and easy to prepare and were perfect for lunchboxes and after-school snacks. However, when a government health warning advised parents not to give ribs to weaning monsters, nutritionists developed this infant-friendly version that's easier on the digestive system.

Sufficient.—for about 30 bones

1 lb strong white bread flour,
    plus extra for dusting
2 teaspoons fast-acting dry yeast
1 teaspoon salt, plus extra for sprinkling
½ cup finely grated Parmesan cheese
¼ cup snipped chives

3 tablespoons olive oil,
    plus extra for greasing,
1¼ cups hand-hot water
semolina, for sprinkling
beaten egg, to glaze

Method.—Mix together the flour, yeast, salt, cheese, and chives in a bowl. Add the oil and measured water and mix to a dough, adding a dash more water if the dough feels dry.

Knead the dough on a floured surface for 10 minutes until smooth and elastic. Place in a lightly oiled bowl, cover with plastic wrap, and let stand to rise in a warm place until doubled in size.

Sprinkle 2 lightly oiled cookie sheets with semolina. Punch the dough to deflate it, then roll out on a floured surface to a 12 x 8 inch rectangle. Cut across into ½-inch strips, then stretch each one slightly and place on a cookie sheet.

Brush with beaten egg and sprinkle with extra semolina. Bake in a preheated oven at 425°F for 15 to 20 minutes until golden. Transfer to a wire rack to cool. Best eaten freshly baked.

CRISPY SKIN WITH INTESTINE SAUCE

Overweight, middle-aged humans traditionally provided the best raw ingredient for this luxurious snack—the skin has aged nicely but still has enough elasticity to make a decent batch. The key to success is patience when it comes to drying the skin; the longer you cure it, the better the flavor and crunch. If you can't wait six weeks, or you don't have a human skin dehydrator, you won't be disappointed with this alternative.

Sufficient.—for 4 hungry monsters to share

7 oz package tortilla chips
1½ cups canned refried beans
1 cup canned black beans,
   rinsed and drained
1 pickled jalapeño chile pepper, sliced
1¼ cups grated Cheddar cheese

Intestine sauce
1 onion, chopped
3 tomatoes

2 garlic cloves, peeled and left whole
1 teaspoon chipotle paste
salt and pepper

To serve
1 avocado, stoned, peeled, and
   chopped
handful of cherry tomatoes, halved
handful of cilantro leaves
¼ cup sour cream

Method.—Make the sauce. Heat a large, dry, nonstick skillet, add the onion, and cook for 5 minutes, turning frequently. Add the tomatoes and cook for a further 5 minutes, then add the garlic and continue to cook for 3 minutes or until the ingredients are softened and charred. Blend to a coarse paste, add the chipotle paste, and season.

Place a layer of tortilla chips in a heatproof serving dish. Mix together the refried and black beans in a bowl. Spoon some of the beans over the chips and scatter with a layer of the chile and cheese. Repeat the layers, finishing with a heavy layer of the cheese.

Bake in a preheated oven at 400°F for 7 minutes or until the cheese has melted. Scatter with the avocado, tomatoes, and cilantro. Drizzle with the sauce and sour cream and serve.

BARELY-DEAD-HUMAN ROLLS

If you're fortunate enough to live close to a human farm that can guarantee a field-to-table turnaround of less than 24 hours, add Human Rolls to your culinary repertoire. Only the freshest cuts will do, as the simple preparation and ingredients rely on the quality of the meat. Swamp dwellers and those of a nocturnal disposition might prefer to try our non-human variation.

Sufficient.—for 30 rolls

1 lb good-quality pork sausagemeat
½ cup walnut pieces, coarsely chopped
2-inch piece of fresh ginger root, peeled and coarsely grated
1 teaspoon black peppercorns, coarsely crushed

1 lb ready-made puff pastry, defrosted if frozen
a little flour, for dusting
beaten egg, to glaze
3 teaspoons harissa paste
oil, for greasing
salt

Method.—Put the sausagemeat, walnuts, and ginger in a large bowl, season with the pepper and a little salt, then mix together with a wooden spoon or your hands.

Roll out the pastry thinly on a lightly floured surface and trim to a 12-inch square. Cut the square into 3 strips, 4 inches wide, then brush with beaten egg. Spread 1 teaspoon of harissa in a band down the center of each pastry strip, then top each strip with one-third of the sausagemeat mixture, spooning into a narrow band.

Fold the pastry over the filling and press the edges together well. Trim the edge to neaten if needed, then slash the top of the strips. Brush the rolls with beaten egg, then cut each strip into 10 pieces and place slightly apart on 2 lightly oiled cookie sheets.

Bake in a preheated oven at 400°F for about 20 minutes until golden and the pastry is well risen. Transfer to a wire rack and let cool for 20 minutes. Serve warm or cold.

BARELY-DEAD-HUMAN ROLLS

It's imperative that the meat used for this dish is fresh,
so it isn't suitable for those who prefer their food in a state of rot or decay.

UNICORN PIES

Free-range unicorns have always been as rare as gold dust but they were worth seeking out for a special occasion. If the price was prohibitive, more patient individuals used to hang around a highway at dusk, where they might be fortunate enough to spot some roadkill. When all else failed, hungry hunters who still wanted pie on the menu would prepare this version, which is very close to the original.

Sufficient.—for 4 pies

1 tablespoon olive oil

8 boneless, skinless chicken thighs, about 1¼ lb, cubed

1 onion, chopped

2 garlic cloves, minced

2 tablespoons all-purpose flour

½ cup white wine

1 cup chicken stock

few sprigs of fresh, or a little dried, thyme

2 tablespoons butter, plus extra for greasing

1¾ cups sliced mushrooms

15 oz shortcrust pastry

beaten egg, to glaze

Method.—Heat the oil in a large skillet, add the chicken, and fry, stirring, until beginning to color. Add the onion and fry until the chicken is golden and the onion softened. Stir in the garlic and flour. Add the wine, stock, and thyme and season with salt and pepper. Bring to a boil, stirring, then cover and let simmer for 30 minutes until the chicken is cooked through. Heat the butter in a small skillet and fry the mushrooms until golden. Add to the chicken and let cool.

Reserve one-third of the pastry, then cut the rest into 4 pieces. Roll out each piece, then use to line 4 greased individual springform pans, 4 inches in diameter and 1¾ inches deep. Roll out the reserved pastry and cut out lids.

Spoon the chicken filling into the pies, brush the top edges with beaten egg, then add the lids and press the pastry edges together. Place on a cookie sheet and bake in a preheated oven at 375°F for 30 minutes until golden. Let stand for 5 minutes, then loosen the edges, transfer to a plate, and remove the pans.

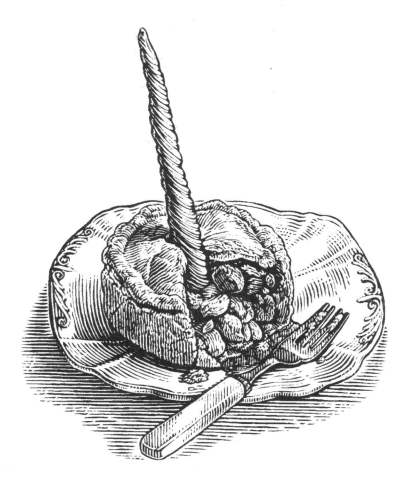

UNICORN PIES

Do not under any circumstances be tempted to use farm-reared unicorn for this dish.
The results will be simply unpalatable.

BAKED EYEBALLS WITH SNOT

If a Cyclops is invited to dinner, be sure to serve baked eyeballs as an appetizer or snack—sight begets sight and a mouthful of the delicately baked morsels will boost the vision of their solitary eye. However, they're not cheap so, if you can't source your own, you might be able to fob off your dinner guests with this cheap—but equally tasty—alternative.

Sufficient.—for 4 monster servings

8 large flat mushrooms, stalks trimmed
8 slices of Taleggio cheese
¾ cup dried bread crumbs
1 garlic clove, crushed
½ cup olive oil
bunch of basil leaves, finely chopped

¼ cup finely grated Parmesan cheese
3 tablespoons toasted pine nuts,
    chopped, plus extra to serve
salt and pepper

Method.—Put the mushrooms on a cookie sheet and top each one with a slice of Taleggio. Mix together the bread crumbs and garlic and scatter each mushroom with a little of the mixture. Drizzle with some of the olive oil and bake in a preheated oven at 400°F for 15 to 20 minutes until golden and crispy.

Meanwhile, mix together the basil, Parmesan, pine nuts, and remaining oil and season to taste. Drizzle the mushrooms with the pesto and scatter with a few extra pine nuts to serve.

SLUG AND SLIME PIES

If a Mummy or a Swamp Creature invites you to supper, chances are you'll be treated to a mouth-watering Slug and Slime Pie. The pastry must be really thick to contain the oozing slime, and the best pies use fattened, farm-reared slugs. If you have a moral aversion to factory farming, let your hosts know in advance—they will probably prepare this slug-free FairFarm® version instead.

Sufficient.—for 8 pies

2 tablespoons butter

1 tablespoon olive oil

1 onion, finely chopped

3½ cups sliced mixed mushrooms

2 garlic cloves, minced

3 sprigs of thyme, leaves torn from stems
plus extra for sprinkling (optional)

1 lb ready-made puff pastry,
defrosted if frozen

a little flour, for dusting

½ cup full-fat crème fraîche

6 oz Stilton cheese, diced with
rind removed

beaten egg, to glaze

sea salt flakes

Method.—Heat the butter and oil in a skillet, add the onion, and fry for a few minutes until just beginning to soften, then add the mushrooms and garlic and fry, stirring, until golden. Remove from the heat, add the thyme leaves, and let cool.

Roll out the pastry thinly on a lightly floured surface and trim to a 14-inch square, then cut into 16 squares. Spoon the mushroom mixture over the center of 8 of the squares, then top with crème fraîche and Stilton. Brush the edges of the pastry with beaten egg, then cover each with a second pastry square.

Press the edges of the pastry together well and crimp the edges, if liked. Transfer to a cookie sheet, then slash the tops with a knife, brush with more beaten egg, and sprinkle with salt flakes and extra thyme, if liked.

Bake in a preheated oven at 400°F for 20 minutes until well risen and golden brown.

MASHED BOOGER TARTS

Fresh boogers used to be a much-loved treat but they were also incredibly messy to eat. To solve the problem of spillages at underling parties, a stay-at-home Cyclops created a booger tart 300 years ago. However, snot intolerance has become a big issue in recent times and many schools and party venues now ban it. This allergy-friendly version has been adopted in place of the original recipe.

Sufficient.—for 16 tarts

1 sheet of filo pastry, 19 x 9 inches, defrosted if frozen
2 tablespoons butter, melted
1 ripe avocado
juice of 1 lime
½ mild red chile, seeded and finely chopped, plus extra to garnish (optional)
1 scallion, finely chopped
2 tablespoons finely chopped cilantro, plus extra to garnish (optional)
salt and pepper

Method.—Unfold the pastry sheet, brush with butter, then cut into 32 small squares, each about 2 inches. Gently press 1 square into each of 16 sections of 2 x 12-hole mini muffin pans, then add a second square of pastry to each at a right angle to the first for a petal-like effect.

Bake in a preheated oven at 375°F for 4 to 5 minutes until golden. Lift the filo cups out of the pans and transfer to a wire rack to cool.

Halve and stone the avocado, then scoop the flesh out of the shell and mash with the lime juice or blitz in a food processor. Add the chile, scallion, and cilantro, season lightly with salt and pepper, and mix together.

Spoon the guacamole into the filo cups, garnish with extra chopped chile and cilantro, if liked. The avocado discolors, so serve within 1 hour of finishing.

MASHED BOOGER TARTS

Booger intolerance is a growing concern, particularly among parents. It's now considered proper to warn your guests in advance should you prepare a booger dish.

SMALL INTESTINE SKEWERS

These are perfect for family picnics. The traditional recipe has been altered somewhat as the skewers take on the flavor of whatever the human victim last ate and, as prey were often captured outside fast-food joints late on Saturday evenings (an easy catch due to alcohol-induced stupor), the quality of intestines dropped dramatically and the original recipe went out of favor.

Sufficient.—for 10 skewers

⅓ cup dark soy sauce

2 tablespoons sesame oil

1 teaspoon Chinese 5-spice powder

¾ lb boneless, skinless chicken breasts,
    cut into long, thin strips

cucumber, cut into strips, to serve

Sauce

¼ cup peanut butter

1 tablespoon dark soy sauce

½ teaspoon ground coriander

½ teaspoon ground cumin

pinch of paprika or chili powder

½ cup water

Method.—Place the soy sauce, sesame oil, and 5-spice powder in a bowl and mix together. Add the chicken and toss together to coat in the marinade. Cover and let stand to marinate in the refrigerator for 1 hour, stirring from time to time.

Thread the chicken, zigzag fashion, onto 10 soaked bamboo skewers (soaking them in warm water for 30 minutes will prevent the sticks from burning while cooking), and place the chicken under a preheated hot broiler for 8 to 10 minutes, turning once, until golden and cooked through.

Meanwhile, put all the sauce ingredients in a small saucepan and heat, stirring, until warm and well mixed. Transfer to a small serving bowl.

Place the bowl of sauce on a serving plate with the cucumber on one side and the hot chicken skewers around it.

SMALL INTESTINE SKEWERS

If you have humans in captivity, alter the flavor of this dish by force-feeding them a food of your choice. It can make for a great flavor-guessing game at dinner parties!

How to Carve a Human

Flesh-eaters are very discerning about their meat and different members of the community favor different human cuts, which is worth remembering when you're entertaining. A skilled human dismemberer will trim and carve the meat for you, so it is easier to prepare. Don't shy away from cheaper cuts—many are coming back into favor and, if properly cooked, these can be as tasty as prime roasts. You should also embrace nose-to-tail-end eating by making use of every last ear and eyeball.

(I) BRAIN
A delicacy for Zombies—best eaten raw or simply fried in belly fat.

(II) EARS (EARWAX)
Ears need to be slow-cooked in order to be edible but larger specimens will yield a good crop of earwax, which is particularly prized by Ogres and Giant Apes as a cooking ingredient.

(III) EYEBALLS
Perfect for snacking, as well as adding to soups and stews.

(IV) NOSE
Giants sometimes add noses to the menu but most other diners will shy away from the chewy consistency of the cartilage. However, snot is a delicacy and you should try to extract every last drop—use a syringe if necessary.

(V) NECK
Vampires particularly enjoy this cut after bloodletting. It needs to be carefully separated from the vertebrae using a very sharp knife.

(VI) RIBS
Perfect for barbecues and dipping; also used as toothpicks by Giants and Ogres. Serve as a rack or individually, depending on the size and appetite of your guests.

(VII) BICEPS
The biceps of body builders are prized by part-mechanical monsters, while slothlike Yetis prefer the leaner meat of bingo wings. Trim away the skin, as this can be tough.

(VIII) HEART AND LUNGS
Avoid fatty or disease-ridden organs and prepare fresh for optimum flavor.

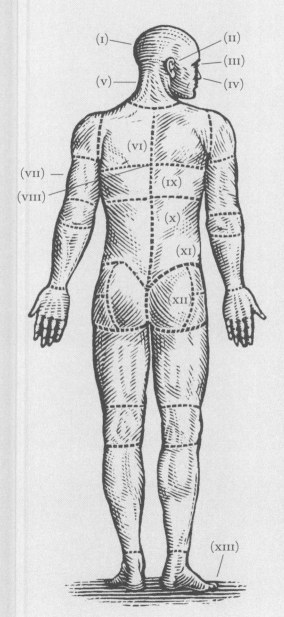

(IX) TORSO
This can be served as a whole roast or cut into chops.

(X) ENTRAILS
These should be served warm, direct from the body—otherwise preserve in vinegar and enjoy pickled when your favorite humans are out of season.

(XI) FLANK
If the human has been exercising to excess the flank can become tough —source from couch-potato shops to ensure a flabby, fat-laden piece of meat.

(XII) RUMP
A well rounded rump will provide a filling meal for a houseful of guests, although Giants will easily consume an entire rump each. Allow the rump to rest before carving.

(XIII) TOENAILS
While fingers and toes are fiddly to eat and yield little meat, nails are a real treat. Try not to dislodge the dirt underneath when you prise off the nails —this adds to the flavor.

SCOTCH EGGS

These eggs were originally prepared with genuine Scottish people, with special care taken to remove all traces of tartan-ware and bagpipes before grinding—even the smallest amount could result in an uncontrollable desire to dance a jig. When genuine Scots were elusive, this tasty alternative was used instead.

Sufficient.—for 4 eggs

⅓ cup all-purpose flour
2 teaspoons mustard powder
1¾ cups fresh fine bread crumbs
5 eggs, at room temperature
4¼ cups peanut oil, canola oil, or sunflower oil

2 heaped tablespoons finely snipped chives
¾ lb sausagemeat

To serve
black pepper

Method.—Mix together the flour and mustard powder in a wide shallow bowl, place the bread crumbs in another bowl, and beat 1 of the eggs in a third bowl.

Boil the remaining eggs in a medium saucepan (3½ minutes for soft yolks, 6 minutes for firmer yolks, or 8 minutes for hard-boiled). Remove, place in a bowl of cold water, and set aside for 5 minutes. When cool, peel the eggs and set aside.

Heat the oil in a deep-fryer or a large, deep-sided, heavy saucepan (the oil should come no more than halfway up the inside) over medium heat to 350°F or until a cube of bread dropped in the hot oil browns in 30 seconds.

Meanwhile, mix the chives into the sausagemeat with a fork. Divide the mixture into 4, then shape each piece into a round patty. Place 1 egg in the center of each patty and gently encase the eggs in the sausagemeat. Roll each in the seasoned flour, then in the beaten egg, and finally in the bread crumbs until completely coated.

Deep-fry the eggs for 5 to 7 minutes or until deep golden brown and the sausagemeat is cooked through. Remove and drain on paper towels. Serve cut in half with freshly ground black pepper.

Note: this recipe has been translated for use by Mummies

BELOVED-FAMILY-PET PIE

The age-old adversary of every Under-the-Bed and In-the-Cupboard Monster, this pie was a great way to make use of over-inquisitive tomcats and mongrels that came sniffing around during a scaring or raid. The more loved the pet the better it tasted, so scarers didn't bother collecting unwanted Christmas puppies or neglected hamsters. Many tribes now suffer with cat dander allergy, so they prepare this version instead.

Sufficient.—for 6 to 8 monster servings of pie

1 lb sausagemeat
1 lb boneless, skinless chicken
    thighs, chopped
4 oz smoked bacon, diced
5 cloves, coarsely crushed
¼ teaspoon ground allspice
small bunch of sage
1 Braeburn apple, cored and sliced
1 egg yolk mixed with 1 tablespoon water

salt and pepper

Hot-water crust pastry
1 cup lard
¾ cup milk and water, mixed half
    and half
2 teaspoons English mustard
3 cups all-purpose flour
¼ teaspoon salt

Method.—Make the pastry. Put the lard and milk and water mixture in a saucepan. Heat gently until the lard has just melted. Stir in the mustard. Bring just to a boil, then tip into a bowl containing the flour and salt. Mix with a wooden spoon until it forms a smooth soft ball. Cover and let stand for 10 minutes until cool enough to handle.

Meanwhile, mix together the sausagemeat, chicken, bacon, cloves, allspice, and plenty of salt and pepper in a bowl.

Knead the pastry lightly, then reserve one third. Press the remaining warm pastry over the bottom and up the inside of a deep 7-inch loose-bottomed cake pan. Spoon in half the meat filling and level it off. Cover with half the sage leaves, then the apple slices, then spoon over the rest of the filling. Level it off and top with the remaining sage. Brush the edges of the pastry with the egg glaze.

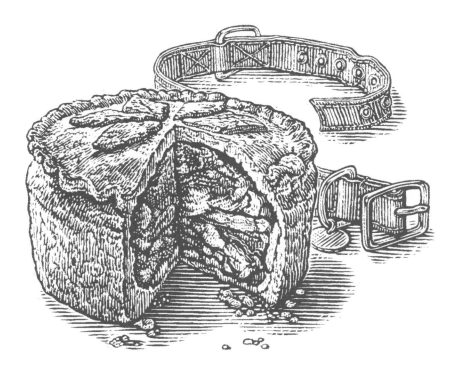

Roll a lid out of the reserved pastry, arrange on the pie, and press the edges together. Trim off the excess and use it to decora the pie. Make a slit in the top of the pie, then brush with the egg glaze. Bake in a preheated oven at 350°F for 1½ hours, covering with foil after 40 minutes, when golden. Let cool then refrigerate for 3 to 4 hours or overnight. Remove from the pan and cut into 6 to 8 wedges to serve.

DRAGON'S EGG TARTS

Larger than an average egg and with added health and healing powers, these tarts used to fly out of monster markets when they were in season. Cliff and cave dwellers were often able to harvest their own dragon eggs but human raiders or anyone with vertigo had to rely on a good mating season for an abundant supply. To avoid disappointment, this mock egg version of the recipe was introduced to great response.

Sufficient.—for 4 tarts

15 oz shortcrust pastry, cut
   into 4 pieces
1 tablespoon olive oil
1 onion, chopped
1 red bell pepper, cored, seeded, and diced
3 oz ready-diced chorizo sausage
2 garlic cloves, minced

¼ teaspoon smoked paprika
2 bay leaves
1 cup canned diced tomatoes
1 cup cherry tomatoes, halved
4 eggs
salt and pepper

Method.— Roll out each piece of pastry on a lightly floured surface until a little larger than a greased 5-inch fluted loose-bottomed tart pan. Lift the pastry into the pans, then press over the bottom and up the inside. Trim off the excess so it stands a little above the top of the pans. Prick the bottoms with a fork and chill for 15 minutes.

Heat the oil in a saucepan and fry the onion, red bell pepper, and chorizo for 5 minutes until softened. Stir in the garlic, paprika, bay leaves, and canned diced tomatoes and season. Simmer gently, uncovered, for 15 minutes, stirring from time to time until thickened.

Meanwhile, line the tarts with nonstick parchment paper, add ceramic baking beans, and place on a cookie sheet. Bake in a preheated oven at 375°F for 8 minutes. Remove the paper and beans and bake for a further 4 minutes until golden.

Stir the cherry tomatoes into the sauce. Discard the bay leaves and spoon the sauce into the pastry crusts. Make a dip in the center, break an egg into each, and bake for 5 to 8 minutes. Remove from the pans and serve warm.

BLOOD, BONES, AND BITS TART

Sticklers for leftovers would always keep the original tart recipe handy. Confident cooks would adjust the ingredients and quantities to suit their pantry. However, those who were afflicted with fussy offspring got fed up with scraping good tart into the garbage can and, rather than let them go hungry, new-age monsters pandered to their demands by preparing this beanstalk-hugging, human-friendly alternative.

Sufficient.—for 6 monster servings of tart

15 oz shortcrust pastry
1 tablespoon olive oil
1 onion, chopped
7 oz raw, trimmed beet, coarsely grated
4 eggs
1 cup milk

1 teaspoon Dijon mustard
small bunch of thyme, leaves torn
    from stems
5 oz goat cheese log, cut into
    6 thick slices
salt and cayenne pepper

Method.—Roll out the pastry on a lightly floured surface until a little larger than a greased 9½-inch fluted loose-bottomed tart pan. Lift the pastry over a rolling pin, drape into the pan, then press over the bottom and up the inside. Trim off the excess pastry with scissors so it stands a little above the top of the pan. Chill for 15 minutes.

Meanwhile, heat the oil in a skillet, add the onion, and fry until softened. Add the beet and cook for 2 to 3 minutes. Beat the eggs, milk, and mustard together in a bowl. Add the onions, some of the thyme leaves, and a generous amount of salt and cayenne pepper. Let stand for 5 minutes.

Put the tart crust on a cookie sheet and pour the beet mixture into it. Arrange the cheese slices in a ring on top of the tart, sprinkle with the remaining thyme leaves, and season with a little salt and cayenne pepper.

Bake in a preheated oven at 350°F for 40 to 45 minutes until the filling is set. Let cool for 15 minutes, remove the pan, and transfer to a plate to serve.

CORPSE QUICHES

For reasons unknown, humans called Lorraine apparently make the tastiest quiches. However, in recent years, this particular name seems to have waned in popularity and Lorraines are now few and far between—those who do exist tend to be older and chewier. These Lorraine-free quiches will still be a talking point at your shindig.

Sufficient.—for 6 quiches

11 oz gluten-free pastry

rice flour, for dusting

1 tablespoon sunflower oil

4 slices smoked bacon,
   about 3 oz, diced

1 small onion, chopped

1 cup grated Cheddar cheese

3 eggs

1 cup milk

1 teaspoon mustard powder

1 tablespoon snipped chives

salt and pepper

Method.— Cut the pastry into 6 pieces, then roll out 1 piece between 2 sheets of plastic wrap until a little larger than a greased individual 4-inch fluted loose-bottomed tart pan. Remove the top sheet of plastic wrap, turn the pastry over, drape into the tart pan, and remove the remaining sheet of plastic wrap. Press the pastry into the bottom and up the inside of the pan with fingers dusted in rice flour. Trim off the excess pastry with scissors a little above the top of the pan. Patch any cracks or breaks with pastry trimmings. Repeat to make 6 tarts. Place on a cookie sheet and let chill for 15 minutes.

Meanwhile, heat the oil in a skillet, add the bacon and onion, and fry for 5 minutes, stirring until golden.

Divide three-quarters of the cheese between the tart crusts and sprinkle them with the onion and bacon mixture. Beat the eggs, milk, and mustard in a pitcher with a little salt and pepper, then pour into the tarts. Sprinkle with the chives and the remaining cheese.

Bake in a preheated oven at 375°F for 25 to 30 minutes until the tops are golden and the pastry crusts are cooked through. Let cool for 5 minutes, then remove from the pans and serve.

CORPSE QUICHES

Vampires will prefer a fresh cadaver to be used for this dish.
Giant spiders will prefer the dried variety.

SWEET GOOEY BAKED BRAIN

Slow-baked and gooey, this was the perfect way to end a meal in the pre-organic era. Cooks needed to gauge the quantities based on their guests—one brain between two for smaller monsters, or around ten brains per Giant. With organic brains being harder to procure, the original dish decreased in popularity and this version took its place. It doesn't have the wow factor of baked brain but a couple of Crispy Baked Rib Bones (*see* page 112) for dipping will help to elevate the dish.

Sufficient.—for 4 monsters to share

10 oz whole baby Brie or Camembert
   (in a wooden box)
¼ cup pecans
3 tablespoons maple syrup
3 tablespoons soft brown sugar
sprigs of thyme, leaves torn from stems

Method.—Remove any plastic packaging from the cheese and return it to its wooden box. Place on a cookie sheet and bake in a preheated oven at 400°F for 15 minutes.

Meanwhile, toast the pecans in a small skillet for 3 to 5 minutes until lightly browned, then set aside. Put the maple syrup and sugar in a small saucepan and bring to a boil. Cook for 1 minute until foamy.

Remove the cheese from the oven and cut a small cross in the center. Drizzle the cheese with the maple syrup, scatter with the pecans and thyme, and serve with plenty of crusty bread.

SWEET GOOEY BAKED BRAIN

If serving Giants you will, as always, need to multiply the portions by at least 10.

SHRIMP SKEWERS

Short humans were traditionally hunted by monster offspring in training camps, as they were easier to catch. They also packed a real flavor punch so were prized for the cooking pot once caught. Humans over 5 feet in height were traditionally used in pies and tarts—the original recipe for these skewers called for prime cuts of diminutive people. When fishing became a more popular pastime than human hunting for certain tribes, this pescatarian variation of the original recipe was introduced.

Sufficient.—for 4 skewers

5 lemon grass stalks
¼ cup sweet chilli sauce, plus
    extra to serve
2 tablespoons chopped cilantro
2 tablespoons sesame oil
20 raw jumbo shrimp, peeled but tails left on

Method.—Take 1 of the lemon grass stalks and remove the outer leaves. Finely slice it and place it in a bowl along with the sweet chilli sauce, cilantro, and oil. Place the shrimp in the marinade, cover, and let marinate in the refrigerator for 1 hour or overnight.

Remove the shrimp from the marinade. Take the remaining 4 lemon grass stalks and remove a few of the outer layers to give you a thin lemon grass skewer. Make a hole through each shrimp at its thickest part using a metal skewer, then thread 5 of the shrimp onto a lemon grass stalk. Repeat with the remaining lemon grass and shrimp.

Place the shrimp skewers on a barbecue and cook for 4 minutes on each side or until the shrimp have turned pink and are firm to the touch.

Serve the shrimp straight from the barbecue with sweet chilli sauce or Intestine Sauce (*see* page 113) for dipping.

FLAYED MINION

The most miserable minions offered up the choicest cuts for the original dish, so they were worked hard for good muscle growth. Unfortunately, this also meant feeding them well, which is why this wasn't an everyday meal. Many communities also chose to keep their captured humans for prolonged servitude—or became fond of them over the years and treated them more like pets than workers—so animal flesh became standard in this recipe, as below.

Sufficient.—for 4

¼ stick butter
4 shallots, minced
1 tablespoon wholegrain mustard
1 teaspoon Dijon mustard
2 tablespoons ready-made
    black olive tapenade
¾ cup hard cider

4 thick fillet steaks, about
    7 oz each
2 tablespoons coarsely ground
    black peppercorns
2 tablespoons crème fraîche
2 tablespoons chopped tarragon
salt and pepper

Method.—Heat the butter in a skillet until it has melted and is beginning to froth. Add the shallots and fry gently for 5 to 6 minutes until softened. Add the wholegrain and Dijon mustards and the tapenade and pour in the hard cider. Simmer gently for 2 minutes, then remove from the heat.

Press the fillet steaks into the black pepper. Cook on a hot barbecue for 3 to 4 minutes on each side or until cooked to your liking. Let them rest on warm serving plates while finishing off the sauce.

Stir the crème fraîche and tarragon into the tapenade sauce, season to taste with salt and pepper, and gently warm the sauce without letting it boil. Pour a little of the sauce over each fillet steak and serve immediately. Try with steamed asparagus, homemade chips, and a dish of mustardy mayonnaise.

Cave Games

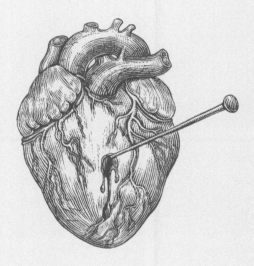

Every good party should include a selection of parlor games. Many members of the community have short attention spans so will need entertaining once the dinner plates are cleared away. It's important to choose games based on your guests—avoid anything fast-moving for Zombies, and dressing-up games are considered inappropriate for Mummies. Likewise, hiding games and Trolls aren't a good match, as they're liable to go into premature hibernation if they remain undiscovered for more than ten minutes.

PIN THE HEART ON THE HUMAN

Draw the outline of a life-sized human on paper. Give one of your guests a human heart to hold, with a pin through its middle. Blindfold your guest, and spin them around a few times. Then ask them to pin the heart on the human. If you have any actual humans dining with you, make it clear to other guests that they're only supposed to pin the heart on the drawing, not on the real humans.

SPIN THE THIGHBONE

Any bone will do but Giants and clawed individuals will find it easier to play with a large bone. When the bone points toward a guest, they must perform a party piece—this could be their specialist skill (howling, fire-breathing, chest-beating, etc.) or a short piano or poetry recital.

ADAM'S APPLE BOBBING

This game makes a real mess so use an old bathtub or wheelbarrow to hold the water and place a plastic sheet underneath. Adam's apples should be purchased from a reputable supplier, or your guests might end up bobbing with a collection of unlanced boils or growths of dubious origin.

PASS THE POTION

This is a great way to use up leftover potions and unwanted Christmas grog. Pass the potion bottle around the assembled group and play some music—when the music stops, whoever is holding the potion must drink it. Be warned, this is a game for serious party-goers.

SNAP

When you suggest a game of snap, human guests will be waiting for you to produce a pack of cards but the monster community will be expecting a pile of bones. The aim of the game is to see who can snap the most bones within a set time frame—usually the time it takes a Zombie to say his or her name.

HIDE AND SHRIEK

This is best played if you've invited Under-the-Bed Monsters to your party, as their scaring abilities are second to none. Ask everyone else to go and hide, then the seeker has to try and petrify as many players as possible.

Hoxton Street Monster Supplies

ESTᴰ 1818

~ Purveyor of Quality Goods for Monsters of Every Kind ~

POTIONS
&
POISONS

INCLUDING
VERY BLOODY MARY
& SATANIC SMOOTHIE

GALLSTONE AND BILE SMOOTHIE

If you're a firm follower of the monster raw-juice trend, add this recipe to your repertoire. It traditionally contained gallstones for an energy burst, while the bile added a deliciously sour aftertaste. It was often drunk as a breakfast-on-the-go or a midnight snack before human baiting. However, many health-conscious communities found that bile sat rather heavily on the stomach, which led to juice guru Dr. Jekyll creating this lighter alternative.

Sufficient.—for 4 smoothies

3 tablespoons crème de cassis or spiced
   red fruit cordial
2 cups mixed frozen berries
1 lb fat-free fromage blanc
1¾ cups milk
1 vanilla bean, split in half lengthwise
toasted sliced almonds, to decorate

Method.—Put the crème de cassis or cordial in a saucepan over low heat and gently heat, then add the berries. Stir, cover, and cook for about 5 minutes or until the fruit has thawed and is beginning to collapse. Remove from the heat and let cool completely.

Process most of the berry mixture with the fromage blanc and milk in a food processor or blender until smooth.

Scrape in the seeds from the vanilla bean and beat to combine.

Fold the reserved berries into the fromage blanc mixture until just combined. Spoon into 4 glasses and serve immediately, decorated with toasted almonds.

HELL BROTH

If you can't shift that winter cold, a flagon of this fiery potion will clear your nostrils and flush the phlegm away in an instant. Brewed in the deepest depths of hell by indentured humans and banished monsters (fangless Vampires, cuddly Giants, water-breathing Dragons, operatic Werewolves, etc.) the agony of eternal damnation is apparent in every sip.

Sufficient.—for 12 fl oz

1 lemon
¾-inch piece of fresh ginger root
1 garlic clove
1 apple, about 3½ oz
1 carrot, about 5 oz
2 celery stalks
3 cups alfalfa sprouts

Method.—Coarsely peel the lemon, ginger, and garlic. Juice all the ingredients together.

Pour the juice into a large glass and serve immediately.

VERY BLOODY MARY

A classic Vampire mocktail—this was often served at celebratory after-bite parties. The taste varied considerably depending on the vintage and caliber of human blood, so this modern version was created to ensure consistency of flavor, and as a standby when hunting packs came back empty-handed. It should always be prepared fresh.

Sufficient.—for 4 Very Bloody Marys

2 garlic cloves, chopped

2 celery stalks, chopped, plus extra
    with leafy tops to serve

1 tablespoon chopped onion

1 lb ripe tomatoes

1¼ cups tomato juice

juice of 2 limes

1 teaspoon celery salt

2 to 3 tablespoons Worcestershire sauce

4 fl oz vodka (optional)

Tabasco sauce, to taste

lime wedges, to serve

Method.—Put all the ingredients, except the vodka and Tabasco sauce, in a food processor or blender and whizz until smooth. Press the mixture through a fine sieve.

Add the vodka, if using, and Tabasco sauce to taste and pour into 4 glasses. Serve with leafy sprigs of celery and lime wedges.

VERY BLOODY MARY

If at all possible, try to find blood from humans called Mary.
You won't regret the extra effort.

UNFILTERED SWAMP CIDER

Swamp dwellers can freely indulge in this natural tonic by dipping a cup into the murky depths and taking a swig. The probiotic craze has led to a number of savvy Swamp Creatures bottling their cider and selling it at local organic fairs. The price rises exponentially with the smell and foul taste, and health-food junkies are prepared to pay a premium for samples bubbling away with natural noxious gases.

Sufficient.—for 10½ fl oz

1 fennel bulb, about 5 oz
1 apple, about 3½ oz
1 carrot, about 5 oz
grated nutmeg, to sprinkle

Method.—Juice all the ingredients together.
Pour the juice into a glass and sprinkle with a large pinch of nutmeg. Serve immediately.

ZOMBIE LEMONADE

It can be difficult for the undead to keep up appearances and this brightly colored cocktail was created to give Zombies an unearthly green glow. It has since been discovered by teenage party-goers from other tribes, keen to impress their buddies by glowing in the dark. Naturally, Under-the-Bed and In-the-Cupboard Monsters should avoid it on nocturnal scaring missions.

Sufficient.—for 8 fl oz

2 lemons, plus extra to decorate
1 cup spinach
1 cucumber, about 11½ oz
sparkling water

Method.—Juice the lemons with the spinach and cucumber.
Pour the juice into a glass, top off with sparkling water, and decorate with a wedge of lemon.

SATANIC SMOOTHIE

A quick fix for those seeking revenge or retribution—this concoction can carry a curse that will see the drinker banished to the underworld at Satan's leisure. You can increase the curse for even greater suffering but this will affect the taste so could arouse suspicion. If you don't add the curse, it makes a very pleasant aperitif at dinner parties and cocktail evenings.

Sufficient.—for 8 fl oz

1 lemon
2 pomegranates, about 1 lb in total
1¼ cups blueberries

Method.—Coarsely peel the lemon. Remove the seeds from the pomegranate by cutting the fruit in half, then holding the halved fruit over a bowl and hitting the skin with a wooden spoon so that the seeds fall into the bowl.

Juice all the ingredients together.

Pour the juice into a glass and serve immediately.

SATANIC SMOOTHIE

CAUTION

Be sure to keep cursed and non-cursed smoothies separate.
Nothing upsets the smooth running of a soirée quite like
a guest being accidentally banished to the pits of hell.

Festivals & Special Occasions

There are a number of important festivals throughout the year—from full moon parties and dragon coming-of-fire rituals, to Day of the Undead and Mummies' Day. We've put together some top tips to help make your special occasion even more special. Whether it's choice consumables, decorative flourishes, or ideas to improve personal hygiene, these can be adapted by every community for every celebration.

ANNIVERSARY

Woe betide any errant husband who forgets an important anniversary. Show your other half you care on your 500th or 1,000th wedding anniversary by presenting them with a bunch of dead roses. If you put them in a vase of swamp water they will slowly decompose and the putrid smell will permeate around your cave, coffin, or lair.

MUMMIES' DAY

Mummies love being singled out on their special day—make it even more special by clubbing together for a new set of bandages or preparing some 1,000-Year Curse-Reverse Cookies (*see* page 45) to try and remove the curtain of evil that hangs over them.

DAY OF THE UNDEAD

If you've been invited to a party by Vampires, Vampire Bats, Zombies, Mummies, Werewolves, or other undead friends, it is customary not to talk about the living world. Instead, stick to topics such as shape shifting, blood gorging, and the upcoming elections for the local Necromancer.

CHRISTMAS

Many members of the community only began to celebrate this human festival at the beginning of the last century but it is now an important day in the calendar. It is traditional to prepare a whole roasted side of human—either ask your local dismemberer to cut and trim it for you, or refer to our guide on page 124.

VALENTINE'S DAY

The older generation eschewed romance for a swift knock on the head with a club. But if you are wooing a Werewolf, dating a Dragon, or courting a Cyclops, this is the day to make your intentions known—send a card with a simple love note or poem:

Corpses are dead
Adipose tissue
Entrails are rancid,
And so are you.

HALLOWEEN

This strange human celebration of all things dead and undead offers the ideal hunting opportunity, as members of the community can freely mingle with their human prey. If you have a sweet tooth you can also steal the sweets that small people collect from their neighbors—perfect as an appetizer before a meal of angst-ridden teenager.

Index

MINISTRY **MS** OF STORIES

TUCKED RIGHT BEHIND HOXTON STREET MONSTER SUPPLIES IN LONDON YOU WILL FIND THE MINISTRY OF STORIES, A WRITING AND MENTORING CENTER WHERE CHILDREN AND YOUNG PEOPLE CAN COME AND DISCOVER THEIR OWN GIFT FOR WRITING.

Through a range of innovative writing programs, and one-to-one mentoring, we help young people discover and then go on to realize their own creative potential. We build confidence, self-respect, and communication skills in both workshops for schools and out-of-school writing clubs.

Then we provide a publishing platform for young writers, so these fresh, exciting voices are shared with the world.

By making writing fun and accessible we help young people find their voices. We challenge their expectations, build their aspirations, and nurture their development, skills, and imaginations.

The Ministry of Stories is a charity. We rely on donations from companies, trusts, and lovely people like you to continue the work we do. Thank you for supporting us by buying this book. Go to ministryofstories.org to learn more about how you could support us.

Registered Charity No. 1138553 | Limited Company No. 07317370

An Hachette UK Company
www.hachette.co.uk

First published in Great Britain in 2016
by Mitchell Beazley, a division of
Octopus Publishing Group Ltd
Carmelite House, 50 Victoria Embankment
London EC4Y 0DZ
www.octopusbooks.co.uk
www.octopusbooksusa.com

Recipe Title Copyright
© Hoxton Street Monster Supplies Limited 2016
Text Copyright
© Octopus Publishing Group Limited 2016

Distributed in the US by Hachette Book Group
1290 Avenue of the Americas, 4th and 5th Floors
New York, NY 10020

Distributed in Canada by
Canadian Manda Group, 664 Annette St.
Toronto, Ontario, Canada M6S 2C8

ISBN 978-1-78472-233-3

Printed and bound in China

10 9 8 7 6 5 4 3 2 1

Commissioning Editor: Joe Cottington
Editor: Pollyanna Poulter
Creative Director: Jonathan Christie
Designer: Alistair Hall at We Made This
Production Controller: Sarah Kramer
Illustrator: Caroline Church
Additional text: Cara Frost-Sharratt

Standard level spoon measurements are used
in all recipes.

Ovens should be preheated to the specific
temperature—if using a fan-assisted oven, follow
manufacturer's instructions for adjusting the time
and the temperature.

This book includes dishes made with nuts and nut
derivatives. It is advisable for customers with known
allergic reactions to nuts and nut derivatives and
those who may be potentially vulnerable to these
allergies, such as pregnant and nursing mothers,
invalids, the elderly, babies, and children, to avoid
dishes made with nuts and nut oils. It is also prudent
to check the labels of pre-prepared ingredients for
the possible inclusion of nut derivatives.

To test if a jam has reached setting point, drop
2 teaspoons of the jam onto a chilled saucer. Let
cool for a minute or two, then push the jam with
your finger. If the top wrinkles, the jam is ready.
Alternatively, if using a sugar thermometer, the jam
should reach 221°F.

To sterilize jars, wash the jars, then rinse well with
hot water, drain, and let stand in a roasting pan.
Warm in a preheated oven at 325°F for 10 minutes.
Alternatively, wash them in a dishwasher and use
as soon as the program has finished while still
warm, but dry.

EST. ROTHERHAM 1148

GRIMM & C<u>O</u>

APOTHECARY

SUPPLIERS OF EVIL PLOTS,
WILD SCHEMES & KITCHENWARE
— SINCE 1148 —

BUY THINGS:

APPROVED BY:

APOTHECARY
TO THE MAGICAL
2 DONCASTER GATE,
ROTHERHAM S65 1DJ
GRIMMANDCO.CO.UK

GRIMM & C<u>O</u>

GOOD 'EALTH. GRAHAM GRIMM.

THIRTEEN PRIZE MEDALS.

SPECIAL APPOINTMENT TO

H.R.H. PRINCE VLAD III (THE IMPALER) & THE ROYAL COURTS OF BELGIUM & ITALY.

HOXTON STREET
MONSTER SUPPLIES
LONDON

THE COLLYWOBBLES

HOXTON STREET MONSTER SUPPLIES'

PATENT AIR-TIGHT CANS

FROM OUR ORIGINAL CANNED FEAR RANGE

Effects a gradual but most certain sensation of the Collywobbles. Corrects and relieves all symptoms of Comfort, Confidence, and Contentment. Most useful in countering cases of Unbearable Smugness. Peculiarly unpleasant to taste, not suitable for those with heart conditions.

SOMBER HARD-WEARING MONOCHROME CAN